Congressional Research Service

Afghanistan: Politics, Elections, and Government Performance

Kenneth Katzman
Specialist in Middle Eastern Affairs

September 20, 2012

Congressional Research Service

7-5700

www.crs.gov

RS21922

CRS Report for Congress ————————————————————
Prepared for Members and Committees of Congress

Summary

Building capacity and limiting corruption at all levels of Afghan governance are crucial to the success of a planned transition from U.S.-led NATO forces to Afghan security leadership. The capacity of the formal Afghan governing structure has increased significantly since the Taliban regime fell in late 2001, but nepotism is entrenched in Afghan culture and other forms of corruption are widespread. Afghan President Hamid Karzai has accepted U.S. help to build emerging anti-corruption institutions, but these same institutions have sometimes caused a Karzai backlash when they have targeted his allies or relatives. At a donors' conference in Tokyo on July 8, 2012, donors pledged to aid Afghanistan's economy through at least 2017, provided Afghanistan takes concrete, verifiable action to rein in corruption. On July 26, 2012, Karzai appeared to try to meet his pledges to the Tokyo conference by issuing a "decree on administrative reforms"—a document of sweeping policy directives intended to curb corruption. Partly because of corruption in the Afghan security forces, on August 4, 2012, the National Assembly voted to remove the ministers of interior and of defense; they have been replaced.

Even though the government is weak, President Hamid Karzai has tried to concentrate authority in Kabul through his constitutional powers of appointment at all levels. Karzai has publicly denied assertions by opposing faction leaders that he wants to stay in office beyond the 2014 expiration of his second term, but he is said to be trying to identify and support an acceptable successor. International efforts to curb fraud in two successive elections (for president in 2009 and parliament in 2010) largely failed and many believe election oversight will be little improved for the 2014 election, although civil society groups are trying to ensure robust competition and electoral fairness.

There is concern among many observers that fragile governance will founder as the United States and its partners wind down their involvement in Afghanistan by the end of 2014. Some argue that the informal power structure, which has always been at least as significant a factor in governance as the formal power structure, will sustain governance beyond 2014 should formal governing structures falter. However, that outcome might produce even more corruption and arbitrary administration of justice than is the case now as major faction leaders gain power. Karzai has failed to marginalize these ethnic faction leaders, in part because they have large constituencies, but he relies more closely on the loyalty of several close, ethnic Pashtun allies, particularly those from the Qandahar area. The non-Pashtun faction leaders generally oppose Karzai's willingness to make concessions to insurgent leaders in search of a settlement. There are fears that a reintegration of the Taliban into Afghan politics will further set back progress in human rights and the rights of women and boost Pashtun power.

Broader issues of human rights often vary depending on the security environment in particular regions, although some trends prevail nationwide. Women, media professionals, and civil society groups have made substantial gains since the fall of the Taliban, but traditional attitudes contribute to the judicial and political system's continued toleration of child marriages, imprisonment of women who flee domestic violence, judgments against converts from Islam to Christianity, and curbs on the sale of alcohol and Western-oriented programming in the Afghan media. See also CRS Report RL30588, *Afghanistan: Post-Taliban Governance, Security, and U.S. Policy*, by Kenneth Katzman; CRS Report R40747, *United Nations Assistance Mission in Afghanistan: Background and Policy Issues*, by Rhoda Margesson; and CRS Report R41484, *Afghanistan: U.S. Rule of Law and Justice Sector Assistance*, by Liana Sun Wyler and Kenneth Katzman.

Contents

Figures

Tables

Contacts

Overview: Historic Patterns of Afghan Authority and Politics

Through differing regimes of widely varying ideologies, Afghanistan's governing structure has historically consisted of weak central government unwilling or unable to enforce significant financial or administrative mandates on all of Afghanistan's diverse ethnic communities or on the 80% of Afghans who live in rural areas. Many communities are separated by mountains and wide expanses that can take days to reach and require traditional modes of transportation. The tensions between the central government and the outlying areas have often mirrored the struggles between urban, educated "modernizers" and the rural, lesser-educated traditionalists who adhere to strict Islamic customs. The Taliban government (1996-2001) opposed modernization.

At the national level, Afghanistan had few, if any, Western-style democratic institutions prior to the international intervention that took place after the September 11, 2001, attacks on the United States. Under the constitution of 1964, King Zahir Shah was to be a constitutional monarch, and an elected lower house and appointed upper house were set up. The parliament during that era never reached the expectation of becoming a significant check on the king's power, although the period from 1964 until the seizure of power by Mohammad Daoud in a 1973 military coup was considered a flowering of Afghan democracy. The last lower house elections during that period were held in 1969. The parliament was suspended outright following the April 1978 Communist seizure of power. The elected institutions and the 2004 adoption of a constitution were part of a post-Taliban transition roadmap established by a United Nations-sponsored agreement of major Afghan factions signed in Bonn, Germany, on December 5, 2001 ("Bonn Agreement"),[1] after the Taliban had fallen. Karzai is the first directly elected Afghan president.

Since the fall of the Taliban, there has also been the growth of civil society, populated largely by educated Afghans, many of whom returned to Afghanistan from exile when the Taliban fell. Organizations and groups centered on various issues, including women's rights, law and justice, media freedoms, economics and business issues, the environment, and others, have proliferated. U.S. and partner policy has been to try to empower these groups as a check on government power and as a guarantor that Afghan democracy will become entrenched.

These newly emerging interest groups have still not been able to displace—or even necessarily substantially influence—the informal power structure of ethnic, regional, tribal, clan, village, and district structures that exercise authority at all levels. At the local level, these structures governed and secured Afghanistan until the late 1970s but were weakened by decades of subsequent war and Taliban rule. Some traditional local authority figures fled or were killed; others were displaced by *mujahedin* commanders, militia leaders, Taliban militants, and others. The local power brokers who displaced some of the tribal structures are far less popular and are widely accused of selectively applying Afghan law and of using their authority to enrich themselves. Some of the traditional tribal councils, which are widely respected but highly conservative in orientation, remained intact. Some of them continue to exercise their writ rather than accept the authority of the central government or even local government appointees. Still other community authorities prefer to accommodate local insurgents, whom they often see as wayward but reconcilable members of the community, rather than help the government secure their areas.

---

[1] For text, see http://www.un.org/News/dh/latest/afghan/afghan-agree htm.

The informal power structure has decision-making bodies and processes that do not approximate Western-style democracy but yet have participatory and representative elements. Meetings called *shuras*, or *jirgas* (consultative councils),[2] often composed of designated notables, are key mechanisms for making or endorsing authoritative decisions or dispensing justice. Some of these mechanisms are practiced by Taliban insurgents in areas under their control or influence. On the other hand, some see the traditional patterns as competing with and detracting from the development of the post-Taliban formal power structure—a structure that, with Western guidance, has generally tried to meet international standards of democratic governance and human rights practices.

At the national level, one traditional mechanism has carried over into the post-Taliban governing structure. The convening of a *loya jirga*, an assembly usually consisting of about 1,500 delegates from all over Afghanistan, has been used on several occasions. Under the constitution, decisions of a *loya jirga* supersede decisions made under any other process, including cabinet meetings or even elections. In the post-Taliban period, *loya jirgas* have been convened to endorse Karzai's leadership, to adopt a constitution, and to discuss a long-term defense relationship with the United States. A special *loya jirga*, called a *peace jirga*, was held on June 2-4, 2010, to review government plans to offer incentives for insurgent fighters to end their armed struggle and rejoin society. Another *loya jirga* was held during November 16-19, 2011, to endorse proposed Afghan government conditions on a strategic partnership agreement between Afghanistan and the United States. However, the constitution specifies who should be delegates at a constitutional *loya jirga*, and, in the absence of elected district councils (whose members are mandated to be included), all of Afghanistan's post-2004 *loya jirgas* have been traditional *loya jirgas*.

Relations Among Ethnicities and Communities

Even though post-Taliban Afghanistan, particularly in urban areas, is modernizing politically and economically, patterns of political affiliation by family, clan, tribe, village, ethnicity, region, and comradeship in past battles often supersede relationships based on ideology or views. These patterns have been evident in every Afghan election since the fall of the Taliban. Most candidates, including Karzai, have pursued campaign strategies designed primarily to assemble blocs of ethnic and geographic votes, although some independent candidates have sought to advance specific new programs and ideas. The traditional patterns have been even more pronounced in province-based campaigns such as those for provincial councils and the parliament. In these cases, electorates (the eligible voters of a specific province) are small and candidates can easily exploit clan and familial relationships.

While Afghans continue to follow traditional patterns of affiliation, there has been a sense among Afghans that their country now welcomes members of all political and ethnic groups and factions. There have been very few incidents of ethnic-based violence since the fall of the Taliban, but jealousies over relative economic and political positions of the different ethnic communities have sporadically manifested as clashes or political disputes.

---

[2] *Shura* is the term used by non-Pashtuns to characterize the traditional assembly concept. *Jirga* is the Pashtun term. The Afghan constitution provides for a constitutional loya jirga as the highest decisionmaking body, and specifies the institutions that must be represented at the *jirga*. If a constitutional jirga cannot be held or is blocked, a traditional jirga can be convened by the president to discuss major issues, although its ability to render binding decisions on proposals is unclear.

The Pashtuns

Ethnic Pashtuns (pronounced POSH-toons, sometimes referred to as Pathans—pah-TAHNS), as the largest single ethnicity, have historically asserted a "right to rule" Afghanistan. Pashtuns are about 42% of the population and, with few exceptions, have governed Afghanistan. The sentiment of the "right to rule" is particularly strong among Pashtuns of the Durrani tribal confederation, which predominates in the south and is a rival to the Ghilzai confederation, which predominates in the east and has historically close ties to Pakistan.

Karzai is a Durrani Pashtun. His cabinet and inner advisory circle has come to be progressively dominated by Pashtuns, both Ghilzai and Durrani, which has largely minimized the advisory input of the non-Pashtun communities. However, Karzai is credited by some observers for consulting with other communities, particularly the Tajiks, before issuing decrees or reaching decisions. The Taliban government was and its insurgency is composed almost completely of Pashtuns. A table on major Pashtun clans is provided below (see **Table 1**), as is a map showing the distribution of Afghan ethnicities (see **Figure 1**).

The Tajiks

Tajiks are the second-most numerous and second most powerful community in Afghanistan. Tajiks are an estimated 25% of the population and constitute the core of the "Northern Alliance" grouping that politically opposes but sometimes works amicably with Karzai. On a few occasions, Tajiks have ruled Afghanistan, although usually for relatively brief periods. One recent example was the 1992-1996 presidency of the *mujahedin* government of Burhanuddin Rabbani, a Tajik (who was assassinated on September 20, 2011). The Tajiks and the Northern Alliance are discussed extensively in this paper.

The Hazaras

Many Pashtuns are said to be increasingly resentful of the Hazara Shiite minority (about 10% of the population) that is advancing economically and politically through education. The Hazaras have historically been looked down upon by the Pashtuns, who have tended to employ Hazaras as domestic workers and other lower and lower middle class occupations. Observers report that many Hazaras, including Hazara women, are earning degrees or pursuing training in information technology, medical, and other highly skilled professions and that they are becoming dominant in many of these higher paying sectors of the Afghan economy. Jealousy of Hazara advancement could have been a factor in the December 6, 2011, bombings of Hazaras in three cities, killing 60, while they were visiting their mosques to celebrate the Shiite holy day of Ashura. A

Pakistan-based militant group, Lashkar-i-Jhangvi, claimed responsibility—possibly in an effort to stir up sectarian conflict in Afghanistan. Afghan Shiite officials said such tactics would not work, as there is no inclination toward sectarian conflict in Afghanistan. However, a rare clash took place between Hazaras and Tajiks in Kabul when a car in procession of Tajiks commemorating the September 9, 2001, death of their historic leader Ahmad Shah Massoud ran over a Hazara bicyclist. The clash was said to reflect lingering Hazara resentment of Massoud's 1993 offensive against then Hazara rivals during the 1992-1996 period of internecine warfare that preceded the accession of the Taliban regime.

The Uzbeks

Uzbeks, like the Hazaras, are about 10%. The Uzbek community is Sunni Muslim and speaks a language akin to Turkish, as well as Dari. The most well-known Uzbek leader in Afghanistan is Abdul Rashid Dostam, who was allied with Soviet occupation forces but later defected and helped bring down the Communist regime in Afghanistan in April 1992. Because of their alliance with the Soviet Union during the occupation period, many Uzbeks in Afghanistan are leftwing and highly secular.

Relative Lack of Attraction to Formal Political Parties

One major issue that connects post-Taliban and pre-Taliban Afghanistan is that the concept of an Afghan nation is not as strong as are affiliation by community and clan. There is a popular aversion to formal "parties" as historically tools of neighboring powers—a perception stemming from the war against the Soviet Union when seven *mujahedin* parties were funded by and considered tools of outside parties. Some of these *mujahedin* parties remain, such as the mostly Pashtun *Hizb-e-Islam* and the mostly Tajik *Jamiat Islami*, as discussed below. However, most of the *mujahedin* era parties have evolved into alternate or broader coalitions. Hizb-e-Islam is a notable exception to that trend, and it does generally still compete in elections as a distinct party. Prior to September 2009, when a new political party's law was adopted, there were 110 registered political parties. However, a September 2009 law required all parties to reregister and to submit 10,000 signatures, spanning at least 22 provinces to verify their support. By the time of the September 18, 2010, parliamentary election, only five parties had completed the new registration process. By late 2011, 38 parties had completed the process, and a total of 21 parties are represented in the lower house of parliament.

Partly because parties are viewed with suspicion, President Hamid Karzai has not formed his own party, but many of his supporters in the National Assembly (parliament) belong to a moderate faction of *Hizb-e-Islam* that is committed to working within the political system. The grouping was reduced somewhat by the results of the September 18, 2010, parliamentary elections. The putative leader of this group is Minister of Economy Abdul Hadi Arghandiwal. A militant faction of Hizb-e-Islam is loyal to pro-Taliban insurgent leader Gulbuddin Hikmatyar; it is called Hizb-e-Islam Gulbuddin (HIG).

Other large parties that do exist, for example the Junbush Melli of Abdul Rashid Dostam, tend to be identified with specific ethnic (in his case, Uzbeks) or sectarian factions, rather than overarching themes. A major party is *Jamiat Islami* (Islamic Society), a party that grouped Tajik leaders during the anti-Soviet war, although many Tajik leaders still identify with the broader anti-Taliban "Northern Alliance." In recent years, key Tajiks have formed broader groupings discussed later, such as the United Front and the Hope and Change Movement. However, these parties do not advertise themselves as "ethnic" parties per se, because Article 35 of the Afghan constitution bans parties based on ethnicity or religious sect.

It was hoped that post-Taliban Afghanistan would produce a substantial number of secular, pan-ethnic democratic parties. Some large such parties have formed, particularly the Hope and Change party of Dr. Abdullah, discussed further below. Another secular, pan-ethnic party, the Rights and Justice Party, was formed by ex-Interior Minister Mohammad Hanif Atmar and other allies in October 2011, also discussed further below. Another party, the Coalition for Reform and Development, has formed in 2012 to try to ensure that the presidential election in 2014 is fair.

Smaller secular parties include the Afghanistan Labour and Development Party, the National Solidarity Party of Afghanistan's Youth, the Republican Party, and the National Congress Party of Afghanistan led by Abdul Latif Pedram. Some parties are left wing, such as the National United Party of Afghanistan, led by former parliamentarian Nur ul-Haq Ulumi, who was in the Communist era military. However, some believe that all the smaller, idea-based parties remain weak because the Single, Non-Transferable Vote (SNTV) system—in which each voter casts a ballot for only one candidate—favors candidates running as independents rather than as members of parties. Moreover, Western-style parties are generally identified by specific ideologies, ideas, or ideals, while most Afghans, as discussed above, retain their traditional affiliations. As a result, many of the parties that have been formed since the fall of the Taliban have centered around personalities rather than broad idea-driven platforms.

Post-Taliban Transition and Political Landscape

U.S. policy since 2001 has been to help expand the capacity of formal Afghan governing institutions, most of which were nearly non-existent during Taliban rule. No parliament was functioning during that time, and Afghanistan was run by a small, Qandahar-based group of Pashtun clerics loyal to Mullah Mohammad Umar, who remained there. Government offices that were functioning were minimally staffed, and without modern equipment, according to observers. There were virtually no checks or balances on Mullah Omar's decision to host Osama bin Laden in Afghanistan during that time. Since 2007, but with particular focus during the Obama Administration, U.S. policy has been to not only try to expand Afghan governing capacity and the ability of the government to deliver services - at the central and local levels - but to push for its reform, transparency, and oversight. However, the formal governing structure continues to compete, often unsuccessfully, with the traditional power structures discussed above.

Establishment of the Formal Afghan Government Structure: Tending Toward Centralization

The 2001 ouster of the Taliban government paved the way for the success of a long-stalled U.N. effort to form a broad-based Afghan government and for the international community to help Afghanistan build legitimate governing institutions. In the formation of the first post-Taliban transition government, the United Nations was viewed as a credible mediator by all sides largely because of its role in ending the Soviet occupation. During the 1990s, a succession of U.N. mediators adopted many of former King Zahir Shah's proposals for a government to be selected by a traditional assembly, or *loya jirga*. However, U.N.-mediated cease-fires between warring factions did not hold. Non-U.N. initiatives made little progress, particularly the "Six Plus Two" multilateral contact group, which began meeting in 1997 (the United States, Russia, and the six states bordering Afghanistan: Iran, China, Pakistan, Turkmenistan, Uzbekistan, and Tajikistan). Other failed efforts included a "Geneva group" (Italy, Germany, Iran, and the United States) formed in 2000; an Organization of Islamic Conference (OIC) contact group; and prominent Afghan exile efforts, including discussion groups launched by Hamid Karzai and his clan, former *mujahedin* commander Abd al-Haq, and Zahir Shah ("Rome process"). The sections below discuss the formation of the post-Taliban governing structure of Afghanistan.

December 2001 Bonn Agreement

Immediately after the September 11 attacks, former U.N. mediator Lakhdar Brahimi was brought back (he had resigned in frustration in October 1999). U.N. Security Council Resolution 1378 (November 14, 2001) called for a "central" role for the United Nations in establishing a transitional administration and inviting member states to send peacekeeping forces to promote stability and aid delivery. After the fall of Kabul in November 2001, the United Nations invited major Afghan factions, most prominently the Northern Alliance and that of the former King—but not the Taliban—to an international conference in Bonn, Germany.

On December 5, 2001, the factions signed the "Bonn Agreement."[3] It was endorsed by U.N. Security Council Resolution 1385 (December 6, 2001). The agreement was reportedly forged with substantial Iranian diplomatic help because Iran had supported the military efforts of the Northern Alliance faction and had leverage to persuade temporary caretaker Rabbani and the Northern Alliance to cede the top leadership to Hamid Karzai as leader of an interim administration. Other provisions of the agreement:

- authorized an international peace keeping force to maintain security in Kabul, and Northern Alliance forces were directed to withdraw from the capital. Security Council Resolution 1386 (December 20, 2001, and renewed yearly thereafter) gave formal Security Council authorization for the international peacekeeping force (International Security Assistance Force, ISAF);

- referred to the need to cooperate with the international community on counter narcotics, crime, and terrorism; and

- applied the constitution of 1964 until a permanent constitution could be drafted.[4]

On December 5, 2011, there was an international conference on Afghanistan in Bonn, marking the 10th anniversary since the 2001 Bonn Conference. The meeting, in part, evaluated governance progress in Afghanistan since the original convention.

Permanent Constitution Adopted, Sets Up Presidential System

A June 2002 "emergency" *loya jirga* put a representative imprimatur on the transition; it was attended by 1,550 delegates (including about 200 women). Subsequently, a 35-member constitutional commission drafted the constitution, unveiling it in November 2003. It was debated by 502 delegates, selected in U.N.-run caucuses, at a "*constitutional loya jirga* (CLJ)" during December 13, 2003-January 4, 2004. The CLJ, chaired by prominent Islamic scholar and former interim Afghan leader Sibghatullah Mojadeddi, approved the draft constitution with minor changes.

The constitution set up a presidential system, with an elected president having relatively broad powers and a separately elected National Assembly (parliament). Opposing too great a centralization of power (which would favor Pashtuns), the Tajik-dominated Northern Alliance

---

[3] Text of Bonn agreement at http://www.ag-afghanistan.de/files/petersberg htm.

[4] The last pre-Karzai *loya jirga* that was widely recognized as legitimate was held in 1964 to ratify a constitution. Najibullah convened a *loya jirga* in 1987 to approve pro-Moscow policies, but that gathering was widely viewed by Afghans as illegitimate.

failed in its effort to set up a prime ministership in which the elected parliament would select a prime minister who would run the day-to-day workings of government. In such a system, the president's powers would be limited. In the constitution, the faction did achieve some limitation to presidential powers by assigning major authorities to the parliament, as discussed below. The Northern Alliance assumed that, in a prime ministerial system, the post of elected president would be held by a Pashtun but, in a tradition of power sharing, the prime minister post would be held by a Tajik or other ethnic minority. The constitution and election system (a two round election if no majority is achieved in the first round) strongly favor the likelihood that an ethnic Pashtun will be president of Afghanistan.

The president serves a five-year term, with a two-term limit (Article 62). There are two vice presidents. The president has broad powers. Under article 64, he has the power to appoint all "high-ranking officials," which has been interpreted by Karzai to include not only cabinet ministers but also members of the Supreme Court, judges, provincial governors and district governors, local security chiefs, and members of supposedly independent commissions such as the Independent Election Commission and the Afghan Independent Human Rights Commission (AIHRC). However, these appointments are constitutionally subject to confirmation by the National Assembly. The president also is commander-in-chief of the Afghan armed forces. In an outcome still debated, at the CLJ, the opposition did not achieve the right of elected provincial and district councils to choose their governors.

The constitution made former King Zahir Shah honorary "Father of the Nation," a title that is not heritable. Zahir Shah died on July 23, 2007.[5] It (Article 58) also set up the Afghanistan Independent Human Rights Commission (AIHRC) to refer cases of human rights violations to "the legal authorities." (See further below on this commission.)

Karzai Elected in First Post-Taliban Presidential Elections in 2004

Security conditions precluded the holding of the first post-Taliban elections simultaneously. The first election, for president, was held on October 9, 2004, missing a June constitutional deadline. Turnout was about 80%. On November 3, 2004, Karzai was declared winner (55.4% of the vote) over his 17 challengers on the first round, avoiding a runoff. He was sworn in to office in December 2004, about one year before the swearing in of an elected National Assembly; he ruled by decree during that one year period.

National Assembly (Parliament) Formation, Powers, and Assertion of Powers

The National Assembly outlined by the constitution consists of a 249 all-elected lower house (*Wolesi Jirga*, House of the People) and a selected 102 seat upper house (*Meshrano Jirga*, House of Elders). The upper house is selected as follows: one-third, or 34 seats, appointed by the president (for a five-year term); one-third appointed by the elected provincial councils (four-year term); and one-third appointed by elected district councils (for a three-year term). Of the president's appointments, half (17) are mandated to be women.

Because of the difficulty in confirming voter registration rolls and determining district boundaries, elections for the 364 district councils have not been held to date. Each district

---

[5] Text of constitution at http://arabic.cnn.com/afghanistan/ConstitutionAfghanistan.pdf.

boundary is likely to be contentious because it will inevitably separate tribes and clans. Until there are elected district councils, two-thirds of the Meshrano Jirga are selected by the provincial councils for four year terms. The lower house is mandated to be at least 28% female (68 people), an average of two for each of the 34 provinces.

Parliamentary and provincial council elections, which were to establish the National Assembly and the provincial councils, were originally intended for April-May 2005 but were delayed until September 18, 2005. The elections were based on a "Single Non-Transferable Vote" System; candidates stood as individuals, not part of a party list. Voting was for one candidate only, although the number of representatives varied by province, ranging from 2 (Panjshir Province) to 33 (Kabul Province). Other examples include Herat, 17; Nangahar, 14; Qandahar, Balkh, and Ghazni, 11 seats each.

The National Assembly has become the key formal institution for non-Pashtuns and political independents to express political opposition to and to exert influence on Karzai. The Assembly has been set up by the constitution as a relatively powerful body that can, to some extent, check the powers of the president, although the Northern Alliance and other Karzai critics say it has insufficient power to brake presidential authority.

Powers of the National Assembly

The lower house has the power to vote no-confidence against ministers (Article 92)—based on a proposal by 10% of the lower house membership, or 25 parliamentarians. Both the upper and lower houses are required to pass laws. Under Article 98 of the constitution, the national budget is taken up by the *Meshrano Jirga* first and then passed to the *Wolesi Jirga* for its consideration. Both houses of parliament, whose budgets are controlled by the Ministry of Finance, are staffed by about 275 Afghans, reporting to a National Assembly "secretariat." There are 18 oversight committees, a research unit, and a library. USAID has helped the Afghanistan National Assembly build its capabilities with a parliamentary assistance program for Afghanistan.

Assertion of Its Authority

After the National Assembly was inaugurated on December 19, 2005, it immediately demonstrated institutional strength. One of its first tasks was to review, and either endorse, amend, or void, the decrees Karzai had issued in the one year he was president and no National Assembly was operating. In March 2006, it achieved a vote to require Karzai's cabinet to be approved individually, rather than *en bloc*, increasing opposition leverage. However, Karzai rallied his support and all but 5 of the 25 nominees were confirmed. In May 2006, the opposition within the Assembly compelled Karzai to change the nine-member Supreme Court, the highest judicial body, including ousting 74-year-old Islamic conservative Fazl Hadi Shinwari as chief justice. The proximate justification for the ouster was Shinwari's age, which was beyond the official retirement age of 65. He was succeeded as chief justice by Abdul Salam Azimi. (Shinwari later went on to head the Ulema Council, Afghanistan's highest religious body, before his death in 2011.)

The process of confirming Karzai's second-term cabinet—in which many of Karzai's nominees were voted down in several nomination rounds during 2010—demonstrates that the Assembly is an increasingly strong institution that is pressing for competent governance. These principles are advocated most insistently, although not exclusively, by the younger, more technocratic independent bloc in the lower house. The Assembly repeatedly voted down Karzai nominees following the contentious outcome of the 2009 presidential election, as discussed below.

The Assembly firmly asserted itself on August 4, 2012, by voting to oust Defense Minister Abdul Rahim Wardak and Interior Minister Bismillah Khan Mohammedi. The move was ostensibly on the grounds of their failure to reduce alleged corruption in their ministries, or to prevent shelling of northeastern Afghanistan from the Pakistan side of the border. However, some asserted the move was an effort to ensure that security contracts were opened to a broader range of bidders. Others felt the vote was a parliamentary overture to Pakistan, because both ministers have been highly critical of that country's hosting of Afghan militants. Karzai said he would abide by the Assembly vote. Wardak resigned shortly thereafter and was made a "senior adviser."

Rivalries Within and Outside Governing Institutions

As discussed above, many intersecting trends—including ethnicity, tribal affiliation, geography, economic interests, and ideologies—determine politics in Afghanistan. These splits manifest within as well as outside Afghan governing institutions, including the National Assembly. Although they largely accept that a Pashtun is most likely to hold the top slot in the Afghan government, non-Pashtuns insist on being—and are—represented at all levels of the central government. Ethnic minorities have demanded, and have achieved, a large measure of control over how government programs are implemented in their geographic regions. Although Karzai has the power to appoint provincial and district governors, in practice he has not appointed governors of a different ethnicity than the majority of residents of particular provinces and districts. One notable exception is the governor of Herat, Daud Shah Saba, appointed in 2011; he is a Pashtun in a province whose major city, Herat, is overwhelmingly Tajik—although many districts of the province outside the city are majority Pashtun. The Independent Directorate of Local Governance (IDLG, which recommends to the presidential palace local appointments) often consults notables of a province on local appointments.

Karzai's Presidential Leadership, His Close Advisers, and Staff

As president, Karzai is advised by what some observers believe is a narrow spectrum of Pashtuns in the cabinet and in his presidential office. Some of them are former members of the moderate wing of the Islamist party Hezb-e-Islam. Among his top aides are his chief of staff, former Minister of Information and Culture Abdul Karim Kurram, who was appointed in April 2011. The chief of staff serves as key gatekeeper of access to Karzai. He replaced Mohammad Umar Daudzai, an Islamic conservative who fought during the anti-Soviet war in more radical Hezb-e-Islam faction Gulbuddin Hikmatyar and was said to be a skeptic of Western/U.S. influence over Afghan decision making. On October 23, 2010, *The New York Times* asserted that Daudzai was the presidential office's liaison with Iran for accepting the approximately $2 million per year in Iranian assistance that is provided as cash. Karzai acknowledged this financial arrangement. Daudzai was appointed Ambassador to Pakistan in April 2011. Another top palace aide is minister-counselor Tajj Ayubi. A top communications aide, Waheed Omar, resigned in August 2011, possibly because of the influence of Hizb-e-Islam supporters on Karzai; he was replaced on an acting basis by Siamak Herawi.

Some of Karzai's top advisers are well-educated and Westernized. For example, Karzai trusts such professionals as French-educated physician—now foreign minister—Zalmay Rassoul and former Foreign Minister and now National Security Adviser Rangin Spanta. Both are Pashtuns.

Spanta, who served in the government during the Soviet occupation era, was foreign minister during March 2006-February 2010, and is said to retain some leftwing views. The National Security Council, headed by Spanta, is located in the presidential palace complex and heavily populated by ethnic Pashtuns. Two other trusted NSC officials (both Pashtuns) are first deputy NSC Adviser Ibrahim Spinzada (a Karzai brother-in-law), and Shaida Mohammad Abdali, the second deputy NSC adviser.

Karzai also surrounds himself with Pashtun tribal and faction leaders from southern Afghanistan, such as Sher Mohammad Akhunzadeh, the former governor of Helmand (until 2005). These personalities reflect Karzai's attempts to exert direct control over his home province of Qandahar and the neighboring large province of Helmand.

An administrative unit that has attracted increasing international attention as a potential center of more organized policymaking is the Office of Administrative Affairs (OAA), referred to by some as the General Administrative Office (GAO) or the "cabinet Secretariat." Some experts say that, particularly under its current head, a Hazara Shiite named Sadiq Mudabir, it is primarily administrative, and without any policy coordination role. However, some say it has taken on an informal judicial role by assessing the legitimacy of citizen, group, and corporate petitions and forwarding those to the relevant ministries for follow-up action. It is a holdover from the Communist era, and contains many longtime bureaucrats. During the 1990s it may have had as many as 1,800 personnel, but has been trimmed during the Karzai era to about 700 staff members. The operations of the unit are funded primarily by the United Kingdom, but U.S. military and civilian officials have been assigned to provide advice and assistance to the office as well.

Some observers assert that the apparatus around Karzai require improved focus and organization. One idea that surfaced in 2009, and which some Afghans still raise, is to prod Karzai to create a new position akin to a "chief administration officer" who can break through administrative bottlenecks. One of Karzai's 2009 election challengers, Ashaf Ghani, was not formally given this role but advises Karzai on government reform and institution building, and manages the transition from the United States and NATO to Afghan lead. Ghani has been part of Karzai's advisory team for all recent major international conferences on Afghanistan, including the December 5, 2011, Bonn Conference. Ghani is considered a top contender for president in 2014.

Karzai's Allies in the Lower House of the National Assembly

In addition to his allies in the presidential palace and the government writ large, as of 2012 Karzai has about 60-70 core supporters, mostly Pashtuns, in the *Wolesi Jirga*. Karzai and his aides hoped to but failed to increase the president's support base in the September 18, 2010, elections, but instead the results caused Karzai's base to shrink by about 20 deputies as compared to his support in the 2006-2011 lower house. Of his lower house supporters, about half are former members of the conservative Pashtun-based Hizb-e-Islam party (the same party as that headed by insurgent leader Gulbuddin Hikmatyar). Others in Karzai's camp in the lower house are followers of Abd-i-Rab Rasul Sayyaf, a prominent Pashtun Islamic conservative *mujahedin* era party leader.[6] As a result, Karzai was unable to engineer the selection of Sayyaf to become lower house speaker in 2011, displacing Yunus Qanooni (Tajik). Neither Sayyaf nor Qanooni was unable to obtain enough votes to become speaker, instead losing to a compromise candidate, Abdul Raouf Ibrahimi, an Uzbek who is perceived as weak.

---

[6] Sayyaf led the *Ittihad Islami* (Islamic Union) *mujahedin* party during the war against the Soviet occupation.

Several of Karzai's supporters in parliament are from Qandahar, Karzai's home province, and from Helmand province. For example, one pro-Karzai Pashtun who was reelected in the 2010 elections is former militia leader Hazrat Ali (Nangarhar Province), who led the Afghan component of the failed assault on Osama bin Laden's purported redoubt at Tora Bora in December 2001. On the other hand, the 2010 elections resulted in the loss in parliament of Karzai cousin Jamil Karzai, and Pacha Khan Zadran (Paktia) who, by some accounts, helped Osama bin Laden escape Tora Bora. A key Karzai brother, discussed further below, is Ahmad Wali Karzai (chair of the Qandahar provincial council), who was assassinated on July 12, 2011.

Karzai Support Significant in the Upper House

Karzai has relatively fewer critics in the 102-seat *Meshrano Jirga* (House of Elder, upper house*)*, partly because of his bloc of 34 appointments (one-third of that body). In 2005, he engineered the appointment of an ally as speaker: Sibghatullah Mojadeddi, a noted Islamic scholar and former *mujahedin* party leader (Afghanistan National Liberation Front, ANLF), who headed the post-Communist *mujahedin* government for one month (May 1992). Mojadeddi resigned in February 2010 and was replaced by another Karzai ally, then deputy speaker Fazl Hadi Muslim Yaar.

Karzai also has used his bloc of appointments to the upper house to co-opt potential antagonists or reward his friends. In 2006, he appointed Northern Alliance military leader Muhammad Fahim to the upper body, perhaps to compensate for his removal as defense minister, although he resigned after a few months and later joined the UF. (He was Karzai's primary running mate in the 2009 elections and is now first vice president.) In 2006, Karzai also named a key ally, former Helmand Governor Sher Mohammad Akhunzadeh, to the body.

Because it is composed of more elderly, established, notable Afghans who are traditionalist in their political outlook, the *Meshrano Jirga* has tended to be more Islamist conservative than the lower house, advocating a legal system that accords with Islamic law, and restrictions on press and Westernized media broadcasts.

Karzai was scheduled to make his 34 new upper house appointments (five year terms) prior to the January 26, 2011, seating of the 2011-2015 parliament. However, Karzai delayed naming his choices while the 2010 election remained in dispute. Because two-thirds of the body serve four-year terms—and the provincial councils that were elected in 2009 were able to appoint their 68 members of the upper house—the body continued to operate even though Karzai had not submitted his 34 appointments. On January 27, 2011, the body reaffirmed Muslim Yaar as upper house speaker. On February 19, 2011, Karzai made his 34 selections, reappointing 18 incumbents and appointing 16 new members to the body. In line with the constitution, 17 of Karzai's appointments are women.

Hamid Karzai, President of the Islamic Republic of Afghanistan

Hamid Karzai, born December 24, 1957, was selected to lead Afghanistan at the Bonn Conference because he was a prominent Pashtun leader who had been involved in Taliban-era political talks among exiled Afghans and was viewed as a compromiser rather than a "strongman." However, some observers consider his compromises as Afghanistan's leader a sign of weakness and criticize him for indulging members of his clan and other allies with appointments. His term expires in 2014 and he is constitutionally barred from running again; he told parliamentarians in August 2011 that he would abide by the constitutional requirement to step down at that time.

From Karz village in Qandahar Province, Karzai has led the powerful Popolzai tribe of Durrani Pashtuns since 1999, when his father was assassinated, allegedly by Taliban agents, in Quetta, Pakistan. Karzai's grandfather was head of the consultative National Council during King Zahir Shah's reign. He attended university in India and supported the *mujahidin* party of Sibghatullah Mojadeddi (still a very close ally) during the anti-Soviet war. He was deputy foreign minister in the *mujahidin* government of Rabbani during 1992-1995, but he left the government and supported the Taliban as a Pashtun alternative to Rabbani. He broke with the Taliban as its excesses unfolded and forged alliances with other anti-Taliban factions, including the Northern Alliance. Karzai entered Afghanistan after the September 11 attacks to organize Pashtun resistance to the Taliban, supported by U.S. Special Forces. He became central to U.S. efforts after Pashtun commander Abdul Haq entered Afghanistan in October 2001 without U.S. support and was captured and hung by the Taliban. Karzai was slightly injured by an errant U.S. bomb in late 2001.

With heavy protection, Karzai has survived several assassination attempts since taking office, including rocket fire or gunfire at or near his appearances. His wife, Dr. Zenat Karzai, is a gynecologist by profession. They have a son, Mirwais, born in 2008.

Family Dealings

Controversy has surrounded his siblings for allegedly profiting from Karza'is presidency. His half brother, Ahmad Wali Karzai, was the most powerful political figure in Qandahar Province until his assassination on July 12, 2011. He was key to President Karzai's information network in Qandahar. Ahmad Wali was widely accused of involvement in or tolerating narcotics trafficking, but reportedly also was a paid informant for the CIA; some of his property has been used by U.S. Special Forces. After Ahmad Wali's death, Karzai appointed another brother, Shah Wali Karzai, as Popolzai chief, and he reputedly has become involved in business dealings in Qandahar that have run him afoul of another brother, Mahmoud Karzai. Mahmoud is reportedly under U.S. Justice Department investigation for alleged corruption. He has wide business interests in Qandahar and Kabul, including auto dealerships, a coal mine, a cement factory, apartment houses, and a stake in Kabul Bank, which nearly collapsed in September 2010. Another brother, Qayyum Karzai, served in parliament during 2005-2008 but resigned in October 2008 for health reasons. He has reportedly been involved in negotiations with Taliban figures on a political settlement. Other Karzai relatives have profited extensively from international contracts, including a $2.2 billion U.S. "Host Nation Trucking" contract. The United States banned contracts to one such firm, Watan Risk Management, as of January 6, 2011; the firm is co-owned by two Karzai relatives—Rashid and Rateb Popal. The Popal brothers reorganized the company as Watan Group and this firm is the local partner of China National Petroleum Company on a $3 billion investment, awarded in 2012, to develop oil fields in northern Afghanistan.

U.S.-Karzai Relations

Karzai has periodically lashed out at what he sees as U.S. and international pressure on him to reduce corruption and ensure electoral fairness. On April 4, 2010, Karzai suggested that Western meddling in Afghanistan was fueling support for the Taliban as a legitimate resistance to foreign occupation.[7] In October 2011, Karzai said that Afghanistan would side with Pakistan in the event of a war between Pakistan and the United States. Karzai has criticized U.S. military night raids, airstrikes, control of detention policies, and U.S. negotiations with Taliban representatives that bypass the Afghan government, although U.S. policy on many of these issues have often adjusted toward Karzai's views. At each downturn in the relationship, top Administration officials have sought to restore the relationship by reassuring Karzai of U.S. support—a main example of which is the May 1, 2012, Strategic Partnership Agreement.[8]

Source: CRS.

---

[7] An exact English translation of his April 4 comments, in which he purportedly said that even he might consider joining the Taliban if U.S. pressure on him continues, is not available.

[8] Dreazen, Yochi, and Sarah Lynch. "U.S. Seeks to Repair Karzai Tie." *Wall Street Journal*, April 12, 2010.

The Opposition: The "Northern Alliance," Dr. Abdullah, and Karzai Opponents in the Lower House of Parliament

Broadly, the political opposition to Karzai (putting aside insurgents) consists mainly of ethnic minorities (Tajik, Uzbek, and Hazara) who fought the Taliban in a politico-military coalition called the "Northern Alliance." Tajik leaders formed the core of the Northern Alliance, and the Tajiks were centered around the legendary Tajik *mujahedin* commander Ahmad Shah Masoud. Members of the Northern Alliance are generally defined by their association with him. Some refer to all Tajik members of the Alliance as "Panjshiris" because many of them are, like Masoud, from the Panjshir Valley north of Kabul. (Masoud, who became legendary for preventing Soviet occupation forces from conquering the Panjshir Valley, was killed by Al Qaeda supporters two days before the September 11 attacks on the United States, possibly in conjunction with that plot.)

Many of these Tajik leaders belonged to the *Jamiat Islami* (Islamic Society) political party, whose leader was Burhanuddin Rabbani (assassinated September 20, 2011, as discussed throughout). As such, Rabbani was technically Masoud's political leader although Masoud was generally perceived as having a larger following than Rabbani, who was from Badakshan Province (not the Panjshir Valley). Rabbani served as president during the *mujahedin* government (1992-1996), and served briefly again as Afghanistan's leader during November-December 2001, before Karzai was inaugurated as interim leader.

Since the constitution was adopted in 2004, leaders of the Northern Alliance have long advocated amending it to give more power to parliament and to empower the elected provincial councils (instead of the president) to select governors and mayors. Such steps would ensure maximum autonomy from Kabul for non-Pashtun areas, and serve as a check and balance on Pashtun dominance of the central government. The leaders of these factions tend to be vehemently anti-Pakistan, which they see as supporting Taliban and other insurgent groups to broaden their influence in future Afghan governments.

In the 112th Congress, legislation introduced October 5, 2011, by Representative Dana Rohrabacher appears to support the Northern Alliance view of decentralized governance by urging that it be U.S. policy to support a decentralized, federal political system that "shifts more power to regions, provinces, and districts and away from a corrupt presidency" and support constitutional reform that provides for election of mayors, police chiefs, and governors.

On the other hand, the Northern Alliance figures and their allies have differences among themselves that has rendered them relatively ineffective as an opposition to Karzai. Many "opposition" figures have often joined Karzai's government in exchange for autonomy or a share of business interests. Examples include Vice President Muhammad Fahim and Balkh Governor Atta Mohammad Noor. A key Tajik figure, Bismillah Khan Mohammedi, was chief of staff of the Afghan National Army during 2001-2010 and was made interior minister in 2010; he is said to have appointed Tajik protégés to key positions in the security forces. (As noted above, Mohammedi was ousted by the National Assembly on August 4, 2012, and a replacement is being sought.)

Other Northern Alliance figures have worked with Karzai on certain issues—a prominent example was former President Rabbani. He agreed in October 2010 to assume the chairmanship of the 70-member High Peace Council—the body that is leading Karzai's effort to reconcile with insurgent leaders. Rabbani's September 20, 2011, assassination by an alleged Taliban operative widened the rift between Karzai and the Northern Alliance adherents who believe that Karzai's outreach to the Taliban has proved naïve and counterproductive. Rabbani's son, Salahuddin, succeeded him. Some suspect the core Northern Alliance concern is that reconciliation will bring additional Pashtuns into government, increasing the Pashtun dominance of government, or that the Taliban will be given control of areas that are at least partly inhabited by members of non-Pashtun minorities. Still, the Karzai strategy of giving high-level appointments to his critics has, to date, proved successful in keeping his opposition divided and off balance.

The Opposition Movements Led by Dr. Abdullah

Although Rabbani was the elder statesman of the Northern Alliance, he was largely displaced in recent years by harder line Tajiks such as the overall "leader of the opposition"—former Foreign Minister Dr. Abdullah Abdullah. Abdullah is about 53 years old; his mother is Tajik and father is Pashtun but his identity as the foreign envoy of Ahmad Shah Masoud causes him to be identified politically as a Tajik. He was dismissed from his foreign minister post by Karzai in a March 2006 cabinet reshuffle and he now heads a private foundation named after Ahmad Shah Masoud.

Dr. Abdullah emerged as Afghanistan's opposition leader after his unsuccessful challenge against Karzai for president in the August 2009 election in which widespread fraud was demonstrated. He is not in parliament but he works to promote his agenda—the cornerstone of which is to establish a parliamentary system in which the National Assembly would select a powerful prime minister—through public statements, in direct meetings with Karzai, and through allies in the lower house, as discussed below. He visited Washington, DC, one week after Karzai's May 10-14, 2010, visit, criticizing Karzai's governance at various think tanks and in a meeting with the State Department. He visited Washington, DC, again in April 2011 and held several meetings with the Obama Administration, while using several think-tank appearances to criticize Afghan governance under Karzai. Dr. Abdullah's representatives have said he is likely to run for president again in 2014.

The pro-Abdullah/anti-Karzai bloc in parliament has gone through several iterations. During 2007-2009, the bloc called itself the United Front (UF), although some accounts refer to it as the "National Front" or "United National Front." It was formed in April 2007 by then *Wolesi Jirga* speaker Yunus Qanooni (former adviser to Ahmad Shah Masoud and Northern Alliance stalwart; he was Karzai's main challenger in the 2004 presidential election) and the late former Afghan President Burhanuddin Rabbani. The United Front included some Pashtuns, such as Soviet-occupation era security figures Sayed Muhammad Gulabzoi and Nur ul-Haq Ulumi, head of the National United Party. Ulumi was not reelected to parliament in 2010.

The United Front bloc underwent changes during 2009-2010 as Abdullah emerged as a national opposition figure, while other Northern Alliance figures reached accommodations with Karzai. In late May 2010, Abdullah created a formal, national democratic opposition party called the "Hope and Change Movement." Running in the September 18, 2010, elections under that name, Abdullah supporters sought to increase their numbers in the new Assembly and hold a commanding position that would enable them to block Karzai initiatives or achieve passage of its own alternative proposals. The 2010 elections results suggest this objective was not achieved, and the number of Abdullah supporters is roughly the same as it was in the previous Assembly—about 60 supporters. This is also a bloc similar in size to Karzai's core support base. On December 22, 2011, 10 political parties launched the National Coalition of Afghanistan, under the leadership of Dr. Abdullah.

Schisms Within the Northern Alliance Grouping

Some Tajik and other figures outside the Assembly are, if not challenging Abdullah for opposition leadership, at least emerging as strong voices. In June 2011, several key Northern Alliance leaders, including Dostam and Hazara figure Mohammad Mohaqiq (see below) joined with former Vice President Ahmad Zia Masoud (Ahmad Shah Masoud's brother) to announce a new opposition group—the National Front of Afghanistan. This group advocates "federalism"—a high degree of autonomy for Afghan provinces, including appointment of provincial governors by elected provincial councils. This differs from Dr. Abdullah's platform of pressing for a parliamentary system. The National Front grouping also is more skeptical of a peace agreement with the Taliban than is Dr. Abdullah and his allies. Even before this new opposition was formed, Ahmad Zia Masoud, as well as ousted intelligence leader Amrollah Saleh (see below), were increasingly outspoken against a potential settlement with the Taliban.

New Opposition Groupings Form

Truth and Justice Party. On November 4, 2011, a new party, the Truth and Justice Party, launched itself as a self-proclaimed reformist party consisting of leaders of all of Afghanistan's various ethnicities. Unlike the coalition led by Dr. Abdullah, this party is in favor of reconciliation with the Taliban. Major figures behind it include Karzai's previous Interior Minister Mohammad Hanif Atmar, who was dismissed by Karzai in 2010, as well as Uzbek leader Abdul Rashid Dostam and Afghanistan Independent Human Rights Commission (AIHRC) Chairwoman Sima Simar, an ethnic Hazara. Taliban era Deputy Justice Minister Jalaluddin Shinwari joined the party as well.

The Informal Power Structure: Other Power Brokers, "Warlords," and Local Faction Leaders

An informal power structure exists outside the formal governing institutions. Karzai has been compelled to work with this informal power structure of well-funded, locally popular, and sometimes well-armed faction leaders, even while heading the formal power structure. Some faction leaders operate in both spheres—holding official positions through constitutional processes while also exercising influence their home provinces—beyond these formal roles. Some are Northern Alliance figures and others are Pashtun faction leaders. Some of these faction leaders—most of whom the United States and its partners regularly deal with and have good working relations with—cause resentment among some sectors of the population—particularly emerging civil society activists—and complicate U.S. stabilization strategy. A number of them own or have investments in Afghan security or other firms that have won business from U.S. and other donors and fuel allegations of nepotism and other corruption.

Still others argue that U.S. policy since 2007 has further empowered local faction leaders or even created new factions and militias that never existed before. A variety of expedient local security initiatives undertaken since 2007, including the Afghan Public Protection Program, its successor the Afghan Local Police Program, Village Stability Operations, and the Critical Infrastructure Police, have created new security organs that sometimes operate without full control by central security organs. These programs are said by critics to have revived the militia concept that was being dismantled by the international community during 2001-2006. Partly because of accusations against these irregular forces created by the United States/NATO, in December 2011 Karzai said Afghanistan would dismantle one of them: the Critical Infrastructure Police, which was created by the Germany-led Regional Command North and was mostly composed of non-

Pashtun minorities. No Afghan government action was taken against the other forces mentioned, which are mostly Pashtun. Some Afghans (particularly the Northern Alliance) believe that the international community's original strategy of dismantling local power structures in favor of a monopoly of central government control over armed force has caused the security deterioration noted since 2006.

Some assert that the Obama Administration's criticism of Karzai has caused him to become ever more reliant on factional power brokers. Karzai's position is that confronting faction leaders outright would likely cause their followers—who usually belong to ethnic or regional minorities—to go into armed rebellion. Karzai has long argued that keeping the faction leaders on the government side is needed in order to keep the focus on combating the Taliban, who are almost all ethnic Pashtuns.

In February 2007, both houses of parliament passed a law (officially titled the National Reconciliation, General Amnesty, and National Stability Law) giving amnesty to faction leaders and others who committed abuses during Afghanistan's past wars. Karzai sent back to parliament an altered draft to give victims the right to seek justice for any abuses. Even though the revised draft contained that amendment, Karzai did not sign the final version in May 2007, leaving the status unclear. However, in December 2009, the Afghan government published the law in the official gazette (a process known as "gazetting"), giving it the force of law.

The following sections analyze some of the main faction leaders.

Vice President Muhammad Fahim

Karzai's choice of Northern Alliance figure Muhammad Fahim as his first vice presidential running mate in the August 2009 elections might have been a manifestation of Karzai's growing reliance on faction leaders, as well as his drive to divide the Northern Alliance. Fahim is a Tajik from the Panjshir Valley region who was named military chief of the Northern Alliance/UF faction after Ahmad Shah Masoud's death. The Fahim choice was criticized by human rights and other groups because of Fahim's long identity as a *mujahedin* commander/militia faction leader. A *New York Times* story of August 27, 2009, said that the Bush Administration continued to deal with Fahim when he was defense minister (2001-2004) despite reports that he was involved in facilitating narcotics trafficking in northern Afghanistan. Other allegations suggest he has engineered property confiscations and other benefits to feed his and his faction's business interests. During 2002-2007, he reportedly withheld turning over some heavy weapons to U.N. disarmament officials who have been trying to reduce the influence of local strongmen such as Fahim. Obama Administration officials have not announced any limitations on dealings with Fahim now that he is vice president. In August 2010, Fahim underwent treatment in Germany for a heart ailment.

Fahim's brother, Abdul Hussain Fahim, was a beneficiary of concessionary loans from Kabul Bank, a major bank that has faced major losses due to its lending practices, as discussed below. The Fahim brother is also reportedly partnered with Mahmoud Karzai on coal mining and cement manufacturing ventures.

Abdul Rashid Dostam: Uzbeks of Northern Afghanistan

Some observers have cited Karzai's handling of prominent Uzbek leader Abdul Rashid Dostam—the longtime head of a party called Junbush Melli (National Front) as inconsistent. Dostam, generally aligned with the Tajiks and part of the Northern Alliance, commands numerous partisans in his redoubt in northern Afghanistan (Jowzjan, Faryab, Balkh, and Sar-I-Pol provinces). There, during the Soviet and Taliban years, he was widely accused of human rights abuses of political opponents. To try to separate him from his armed followers, in 2005 Karzai appointed him to the post of chief of staff of the armed forces. On February 4, 2008, Afghan police surrounded Dostam's villa in Kabul in response to reports that he attacked an ethnic Turkmen rival, but Karzai did not order his arrest for fear of stirring unrest among Dostam's followers. To try to resolve the issue without stirring unrest, in December 2008 Karzai purportedly reached an agreement with Dostam under which he resigned as chief of staff and went into exile in Turkey in exchange for the dropping of any case against him.[9]

Dostam returned to Afghanistan on August 16, 2009, and subsequently held a large pro-Karzai election rally in his home city of Shebergan. Part of his intent in supporting Karzai was to limit the influence of a strong rival figure in the north, Balkh Province Governor Atta Mohammad Noor, see below. Noor is a Tajik but, under a 2005 compromise with Karzai, is in control of a province that is inhabited by many Uzbeks. Dostam's support apparently helped Karzai carry several provinces in the north in the 2009 election, including Jowzjan, Sar-i-Pol, and Faryab. In January 2010, he was restored to his previous, primarily honorary, position of chief of staff of the armed forces. Although Dostam was not nominated to a cabinet post in 2010, two members of his Junbush Melli party were—although they were voted down by the National Assembly because the Assembly did not want to confirm partisan activists in the cabinet.

Dostam's failure to secure posts for his allies could account for his decision to join the opposition grouping formed in June 2011, discussed above. In June 2012, the Karzai government launched a prosecution of Dostam for allegedly insisting the China National Petroleum Co. (CNPC) hire Dostam loyalists to security and other jobs on their oil development project in northern Afghanistan. However, Dostam and those close to him alleged that the prosecution was a Karzai effort to favor his relatives' firm, Watan Group, which is the partner of CNPC on the project and which is therefore in line to provide security and other services to the development. Dostam continues to alternate his time between Afghanistan and Turkey; he is said to be suffering from health problems.

Dostam's reputation is further clouded by his actions during the U.S.-backed war against the Taliban. On July 11, 2009, the *New York Times* reported that allegations that Dostam had caused the death of several hundred Taliban prisoners during the major combat phase of OEF (late 2001) were not investigated by the Bush Administration. In responding to assertions that there was no investigation of the *Dasht-e-Laili* massacre because Dostam was a U.S. ally,[10] President Obama said any allegations of violations of laws of war need to be investigated. Dostam responded to Radio Free Europe/Radio Liberty (which carried the story) that only 200 Taliban prisoners died and primarily because of combat and disease, not intentional actions of his forces.

---

[9] CRS e-mail conversation with a then National Security aide to President Karzai, December 2008.

[10] This is the name of the area where the Taliban prisoners purportedly died and were buried in a mass grave.

Atta Mohammad Noor: Balkh Province

Atta Mohammad Noor, another figure generally considered part of the Northern Alliance, has been the governor of Balkh Province, whose capital is the vibrant city of Mazar-e-Sharif, since 2005. Mazar-e-Sharif is one of the four cities to be transitioned to Afghan security leadership in June 2011. It is unique in that 60% of the residents of the city have access to electricity 24 hours per day, a far higher percentage than most other cities in Afghanistan, and higher even than Kabul. He is an ethnic Tajik and former *mujahedin* commander who openly endorsed Dr. Abdullah in the 2009 presidential election. However, Karzai has kept Noor in place because he has kept the province secure, allowing Mazar-e-Sharif to become a major trading hub, and because displacing him could cause ethnic unrest. Observers say that Noor exemplifies the local potentate, brokering local security and business arrangements that enrich Noor and his allies while ensuring stability and prosperity.[11] Some reports say that he commands two private militias in the province that, in at least two districts (Chimtal and Charbolak), outnumber official Afghan police, and which prompt complaints of abuses (land seizures) by the province's Pashtuns.

Mohammed Mohaqiq: Hazara Stalwart

Another faction leader is Mohammad Mohaqiq, a Hazara leader. During the war against the Soviet Union and then Taliban, Mohaqiq was a commander of Hazara fighters in and around Bamiyan Province, and a major figure in the Hazara Shiite Islamist party Hezb-e-Wahdat (Unity Party). The party was supported by Iran during those periods.

Currently, Mohaqiq is aligned with Dostam and hardline Tajik figures. He joined these figures in forming the National Front of Afghanistan in June 2011. In July 2012, Mohaqiq demanded Karzai fire the head of the Academy of Sciences for publishing a new national almanac that Mohaqiq said overstated the percentage of Pashtuns in Afghanistan at 60%. Karzai fired the Academy head and three others at that institution. Another major Hazara figure, Karim Khalili, tends to work with Karzai and has served as his second vice president through Karzai's two terms as president.

Isma'il Khan: Western Afghanistan/Herat

Another Northern Alliance strongman that Karzai has sought to simultaneously engage and weaken is prominent Tajik political leader and former Herat Governor Ismail Khan. Herat is one of the four cities that was transitioned to Afghan security leadership in July 2011. In 2006, Karzai appointed him minister of energy and water, taking him away from his political base in the west. However, Khan remains influential in the west, and maintaining ties to Khan helped Karzai win Tajik votes in Herat Province that might otherwise have gone to Dr. Abdullah. Certified results showed Karzai winning that province, indicating that the deal with Khan was helpful to Karzai.

Still, Khan is said to have several opponents in Herat, and a bombing there on September 26, 2009, narrowly missed his car. U.S. officials purportedly preferred that Khan not be in the cabinet because of his record as a local potentate, although some U.S. officials credit him with cooperating with the privatization of the power sector of Afghanistan. Karzai renominated Khan in his ministry post on December 19, 2009, causing purported disappointment by parliamentarians and western donor countries who want Khan and other faction leaders

---

[11] Gall, Carlotta, "In Afghanistan's North, Ex-Warlord Offers Security." *New York Times*, May 17, 2010.

weakened. His renomination was voted down by the National Assembly but he remains in an acting capacity. Additional questions about Khan were raised in November 2010 when Afghan television broadcast audio files purporting to contain Khan insisting that election officials alter the results of the September 18, 2010, parliamentary elections.[12] Khan is on the High Peace Council that is the main body overseeing the reconciliation process with Taliban leaders.

Helmand Province Power Brokers

Karzai's relationship with a Pashtun strongman, Sher Mohammad Akhundzadeh, demonstrates the dilemmas facing Karzai in governing Afghanistan. Akhunzadeh was a close associate of Karzai when they were in exile in Quetta, Pakistan, during Taliban rule. Karzai appointed him governor of Helmand after the fall of the Taliban, but in 2005, Britain demanded he be removed for his abuses and reputed facilitation of drug trafficking, as a condition of Britain taking security control of Helmand. Karzai reportedly has sought to reappoint Akhundzadeh, who Karzai believes was more successful against militants in Helmand using his local militiamen than Britain has been with its more than 9,500 troops there. However, Britain and the United States have prevailed on Karzai not to remove the current governor, Ghulab Mangal, who has won wide praise for his successes establishing effective governance in Helmand (discussed further under "Expanding Local (Subnational) Governance") and for reducing poppy cultivation there. Akhunzadeh attempted to deliver large numbers of votes for Karzai in Helmand, although turnout in that province was very light partly due to Taliban intimidation of voters.

An Akhunzadeh ally, Abdul Wali Khan (nicknamed "Koka"), was similarly removed by British pressure in 2006 as police chief of Musa Qala district of Helmand. However, the Afghan government insisted on—and obtained—his reinstatement a few years later and his militia followers subsequently became the core of the 220-person police force in the district. Koka is mentioned in a congressional report as accepting payments from security contractors who are working under the U.S. Department of Defense's (DOD's) "Host National Trucking" contract that secures U.S. equipment convoys. Koka allegedly agreed to secure the convoys in exchange for the payments.[13]

Karzai Family: Qandahar Province

Governing Qandahar, a province of about 2 million, of whom about half live in Qandahar city, is a sensitive issue in Kabul because of President Karzai's active political interest in his home province. Qandahar governance is particularly crucial to ongoing U.S. military-led operations to increase security in surrounding districts, giving the July 12, 2011, assassination of Karzai's half brother, Ahmad Wali Karzai, crucial significance.

Ahmad Wali was chair of the Qandahar provincial council, a post with relatively limited formal power, but he was always more powerful than any appointed governor of Qandahar. President Karzai frequently rotated the governors of Qandahar to ensure that none of them would impinge on Ahmad Wali's authority. Perceiving him as the key power broker in the province, many

---

[12] Partlow, Joshua, "Audio Files Raise New Questions About Afghan Elections." *Washington Post*, November 11, 2010.

[13] House of Representatives. Subcommittee on National Security and Foreign Affairs, Committee on Oversight and Government Reform. "Warlord, Inc.: Extortion and Corruption Along the U.S. Supply Chain in Afghanistan." Report of the Majority Staff, June 2010.

constituents and interest groups met him each day to request his interventions on their behalf. Qandahar governance suffered an additional blow on July 27, 2011, when the appointed mayor of Qandahar city, Ghulam Haider Hamidi, was assassinated. Hamidi was an Afghan American accountant by training.

Before Ahmad Wali's assassination, U.S. officials had been trying to bolster the clout of the appointed Qandahar governor, Tooryalai Wesa by supporting Wesa's efforts to equitably distribute development funds and build local governing structures.[14] Karzai had appointed Wesa—a Canadian-Afghan academic—in December 2008, perhaps hoping that his ties to Canada would convince Canada to continue its mission in Qandahar beyond 2011. That did not succeed.

The international community expected, and hoped, that the death of Ahmad Wali Karzai would further empower Governor Wesa. However, Karzai quickly installed another of his brothers, Shah Wali Karzai, as head of the Popolzai clan and informal Qandahar power broker after Ahmad Wali's death. Shah Wali at first lacked the acumen and clout of Ahmad Wali, but reports in mid-2012 say he has become highly influential, while also becoming involved in significant business dealings in the province that continue to cast aspersions on the motives and actions of the Karzai family. Karzai has also used former Qandahar governor Asadullah Khalid (confirmed in September 2012 as the new intelligence director, as discussed below) as an informal envoy in the province.

Another power center is Qandahar's police chief, Colonel Abdul Razziq. He is perceived as having increasing weight, as well as a reputation for corruption, including siphoning off customs revenues at the key Spin Boldak crossing from Pakistan. He was appointed to his current post in March 2011 when his predecessor was killed in an insurgent attack. Razziq's convoy was attacked in September 2012, and he was injured, but not severely.

Ghul Agha Shirzai: Eastern Afghanistan/Nangarhar

A key gubernatorial appointment has been Ghul Agha Shirzai as governor of Nangarhar. He is a Pashtun from the powerful Barakzai clan based in Qandahar Province, previously serving as governor of that province, where he reportedly continued to exercise influence in competition with Ahmad Wali Karzai. Ahmad Wali Karzai's death on July 12, 2011, could prompt Sherzai and his allies to assert themselves in the province, possibly by trying to convince Karzai to make him Qandahar governor again.

In Nangarhar, Sherzai is generally viewed as an interloper. But, much as has Noor in Balkh, Shirzai has exercised effective leadership, particularly in curbing poppy cultivation there. At the same time, Shirzai is also widely accused of arbitrary action against political or other opponents, and he reportedly does not remit all the customs duties collected at the Khyber Pass/Torkham crossing to the central government. He purportedly uses the funds for the benefit of the province, not trusting that funds remitted to Kabul would be spent in the province. As noted above, Shirzai had considered running against Karzai in 2009 but then opted not to run as part of a reported "deal" that yielded unspecified political and other benefits for Shirzai.

---

[14] Partlow, Joshua, "U.S. Seeks to Bolster Kandahar Governor, Upend Power Balance," *Washington Post*, April 29, 2010.

Emerging Power Centers: Civil Society and "Independent" Activists

Another interest group has emerged since the fall of the Taliban—a product of Afghanistan's increasing modernity and the effect of international policies to promote democracy and human rights. Civil society activists and "independents" in the National Assembly and other institutions are a growing force in Afghan politics. They are generally intellectuals, businessmen, and women's activists who have become more prominent and outspoken since the ousting of the Taliban regime, with easy access to media outlets. However, although they are articulate and backed by some democracy-oriented international NGOs, these civil society leaders have struggled against traditional faction leaders to exert influence over policy. U.S.-based International Republican Institute (IRI) has helped train the independents in the National Assembly; the National Democratic Institute (NDI) has assisted the more established factions.

Of the independents that were present in the 2005-2010 parliament, one, the 45-year-old Malalai Joya (Farah Province), was a leading critic of war-era faction leaders. In May 2007 the lower house voted to suspend her for this criticism for the duration of her term and she did not seek reelection in 2010. Ms. Fawzia Koofi, a one time a deputy lower house speaker and declared presidential candidate for 2014, also remains in the Assembly and an outspoken leader on Afghan women's rights.

Others in this independent camp have included Ms. Fauzia Gailani (Herat Province, not returned to parliament); Ms. Shukria Barekzai, chairwoman of the lower house Defense Committee during 2011; and Mr. Ramazan Bashardost, a former Karzai minister who champions parliamentary powers and has established a "complaints tent" near the parliament building to highlight and combat official corruption. (He ran for president in the 2009 elections on an anti-corruption platform and drew an unexpectedly large amount of votes.) Bashardost was returned to parliament in the September 2010 election and may run again in 2014.

Some other leading independents are present in the 2011-2015 lower house. They include Rafiq Shahir from Herat, a well-known civil-society activist; Dr. Saleh Seljuki; and Ahmad Behzad (all from Herat). Other independents reelected include Shakiba Hashemi and Khalid Pashtun, both from Qandahar.

Ethnic and Factional Cooperation in the Security Sector

The security organs are considered an arena where Pashtuns, Tajiks, and others, of all factional affiliations, have worked together relatively well. The National Directorate for Security (NDS, the intelligence directorate) was headed by a non-Pashtun (Amrollah Saleh, a Tajik) during 2006-2010, although he was dismissed on June 6, 2010, by Karzai for disagreements over whether and how to engage insurgent leaders in political settlement negotiations. He was replaced by a Pashtun, Rehmat Nabil, who had no previous intelligence experience but is perceived as more consultative than was Saleh. Still, he inherited a service dominated by Tajiks (although some left when Saleh was ousted) and by a mix of personnel that served during the Soviet occupation era (the service was then called Khad), and in the *mujahedin* government of 1992-1996. During 2002-2007, the Central Intelligence Agency reportedly paid for all of the NDS budget.[15]

Perhaps to preserve the tradition of ethnic balance in the security sector of government, the chief of staff of the Afghan National Army, Bismillah Khan Mohmmadi (a Tajik), was named interior minister on June 26, 2010. He replaced Mohammad Hanif Atmar, a Pashtun, who was fired the same day and on roughly the same grounds as Saleh (see above for Atmar's role in an opposition party formed in November 2011). By all accounts, Khan is widely respected, even among Pashtuns. The security ministries tend to have key deputies who are of a different ethnicity than the minister or top official. As noted above, Khan, as well as Defense Minister Wardak, was removed by the National Assembly on August 4, 2012.

Some observers assert that Tajiks continue to control many of the command ranks of the Afghan security institutions, giving Pashtuns only a veneer of control of these organizations. U.S. commanders in Afghanistan say the composition of the national security forces—primarily the Afghan National Army and Afghan National Police—has been brought broadly into line with the population. However, Pashtuns from the south (Durranis) remain underrepresented, in part because of the fears that insurgents might target their relatives if they join the security forces. Many of the Pashtuns in the security forces are from the Jalalabad area and are of the Ghilzai Pashtun tribal confederation that is prevalent there and elsewhere in the east.

New Security Chiefs Appointed in September 2012

On September 3, Karzai nominated (1) Bismillah Khan Mohammedi, a prominent Tajik, to become Defense Minister; (2) Gen. Ghulam Mujtaba Patang, a Pashtun, to be Interior Minister; (3) Minister of Tribal and Border Affairs Asadullah Khalid, also a Pashtun, to switch posts and become head of the National Directorate of Security (intelligence directorate); and (4) Azizullah Din Mohammad to take over Khalid's ministry. Some expected the National Assembly to vote down Bismillah Khan because the Assembly had ousted him from the Interior Minister post only one month earlier. Asadullah Khalid's confirmation was similarly in doubt because of allegations he backed torture of prisoners as governor of Qandahar province. Since leaving that office in 2008, Khalid had emerged as a powerful intermediary for Karzai, particularly as an informal envoy in Qandahar following the 2011 assassination of Karzai's brother Ahmad Wali. And Khalid has good relations with the Northern Alliance grouping, boosting his political support in the National Assembly. Patang, a longtime police official, most recently has headed the Afghan Public Protection Force, which is taking over security for diplomats and development projects from private security forces, but has been slow to develop. Despite the concerns above, on September 16, 2012, the National Assembly approved all three security posts overwhelmingly, but voted down Din Mohammad. The approvals retained the rough factional balance in the security sector. Patang's confirmation represents the appointment of the first professional police officer to rise to the post of Interior Minister.

---

[15] Filkins, Dexter, and Mark Mazzetti. "Key Karzai Aide in Graft Inquiry is Linked to C.I.A." *New York Times*, August 26, 2010.

Elections in 2009 and 2010 Widened Political Schisms

Elections are widely considered a key harbinger of the durability and extent of Afghanistan's political development—and a barometer of the degree to which factional, political, ethnic, and sectarian rivalries can be reduced. The 2009 presidential and provincial elections were the first post-Taliban elections run by the Afghan government itself in the form of the Afghanistan Independent Electoral Commission. Donors, including the United States, invested almost $500 million in 2009 to improve the capacity of the Afghan government to conduct the elections.[16] Both it and the September 2010 National Assembly elections were flawed, as discussed below, and widened rather than reduced differences between Karzai and his opponents.

2009 Presidential Election

The 2009 election was plagued, from the start, by assertions of a lack of credibility of the Independent Elections Commission. Its commissioners, including then-Chairman Azizullah Ludin, were selected by, and many were politically close to, Karzai. As a check and balance to ensure electoral credibility, there was also a U.N.-appointed Elections Complaints Commission (ECC) that reviewed fraud complaints. Under the 2005 election law, there were three ECC seats for foreign nationals, appointed by the Special Representative of the U.N. Secretary General/head of U.N. Assistance Mission–Afghanistan, UNAMA. The two Afghans on the ECC governing council[17] were appointed by the Supreme Court and Afghanistan Independent Human Rights Commission, respectively.

Disputes first erupted over the election date. On February 3, 2009, Afghanistan's Independent Election Commission (IEC) set August 20, 2009, as the election date (a change from a date mandated by Article 61 of the Constitution as April 21, 2009, in order to allow at least 30 days before Karzai's term expired on May 22, 2009). The IEC decision on the latter date cited Article 33 of the Constitution as mandating universal accessibility to the voting—and saying that the April 21 date was precluded by difficulties in registering voters, printing ballots, training staff, advertising the elections, and the dependence on international donor funding, in addition to the security questions.[18] His opponents (led by Dr. Abdullah) insisted that Karzai's presidency ended May 22, 2009, and that a caretaker government should run Afghanistan until elections. The IEC reaffirmed on March 4, 2009, that the election would be held on August 20, 2009. Karzai argued that the Constitution does not provide for any transfer of power other than in case of election or death of a president. The Afghan Supreme Court backed that decision on March 28, 2009, and the Obama Administration publicly backed these rulings.

Election Modalities and Processes

Despite the political dispute between Karzai and his opponents, enthusiasm among the public appeared high in the run-up to the election. Registration, which updated 2005 voter rolls, was conducted during October 2008-March 2009. About 4.5 million new voters registered, and about 17 million total Afghans were registered. However, there were widespread reports of registration

---

[16] Report by the Special Inspector General for Afghanistan Reconstruction (SIGAR), September 9, 2010.

[17] ECC website, http://www.ecc.org.af/en/.

[18] Statement of the Independent Election Commission Secretariat, February 3, 2009, provided to CRS by a Karzai national security aide.

fraud (possibly half of all new registrants), with some voters registering on behalf of women who do not, by custom, show up at registration sites, and others selling registration cards.

Presidential candidates filed to run during April 24—May 8, 2009. A total of 44 registered to run for president, of which three were disqualified for various reasons, leaving a field of 41 (later reduced to 32 after several dropped out). In the provincial elections, 3,200 people competed for 420 seats nationwide. Although about 80% of the provincial council candidates ran as independents, some of Afghanistan's parties, including Hezb-i-Islam, fielded multiple candidates in several different provinces. The provincial elections component of the election received little attention, in part because the role of these councils is unclear. About 200 women competed for the 124 seats reserved for women (29%) on the provincial councils, although in two provinces (Qandahar and Uruzgan) there were fewer women candidates than reserved seats. In Kabul Province, 524 candidates competed for the 29 seats of the council.

The European Union, supported by the Organization for Security and Cooperation in Europe (OSCE) sent a few hundred observers, and the International Republican Institute and National Democratic Institute sent observers as well. About 8,000 Afghans assisted the observation missions, according to the U.N. Nations Development Program.

Security was a major issue for all the international actors supporting the Afghan elections process, amid open Taliban threats against Afghans who vote. In the first round, about 7,000 polling centers were to be established (with each center having multiple polling places, totaling about 29,000), but, of those, about 800 were deemed too unsafe to open, most of them in restive Helmand and Qandahar provinces. A total of about 6,200 polling centers opened on election day.

The total cost of the Afghan elections in 2009 were about $300 million. Other international donors contributing funds to close the gap left by the U.S. contribution of about $175 million.

The Political Contest and Campaign

The presidential competition took shape in May 2009. In the election-related deal-making,[19] Karzai obtained an agreement from Fahim to run as his first vice presidential running mate. In doing so, Karzai showed the UF opposition grouping to be split. Karzai, Fahim, and incumbent second Vice President Karim Khalili (a Hazara) registered their ticket on May 4, 2009, just before Karzai left to visit the United States. Karzai convinced several prominent Pashtuns not to run, including Ghul Agha Shirzai, a member of the powerful Barakzai clan; and Anwar al-Haq Ahady, the former finance minister and Central Bank governor. Anti-Karzai Pashtuns failed to coalesce around one challenger, such as Former Interior Minister Ali Jalali and former Finance Minister (2002-2004) and then Karzai critic Ashraf Ghani. Ghani decided to run without Jalali or prominent representation from other ethnicities in his vice presidential slots.

The UF had difficulty forging a united challenge to Karzai. Dr. Abdullah registered to run with UF backing. His running mates were Dr. Cheragh Ali Cheragh, a Hazara who did poorly in the 2004 election, and a little known Pashtun, Homayoun Wasefi.

---

[19] Some of the information in this section obtained in CRS interviews with a Karzai national security aide, December 2008.

Karzai went into the election as a clear favorite, but the key question was whether he would win in the first round (more than 50% of the vote). Although Karzai was criticized for a campaign that relied on reaching out to traditional leaders, he did participate in at least one publicly broadcast debate (August 16, 2009, on state-run Radio Television-Afghanistan, RTA) with two of his rivals (Abdullah did not participate). Dr. Abdullah campaigned extensively in his key base in the north and west, which are populated mainly by Tajiks, but he did campaign in some Pashtun-dominated areas. Both Karzai and Abdullah held large rallies in Kabul and elsewhere.

Ghani had spent much time in the United States and Europe and many average Afghans viewed him as out of touch. Focusing on urban voters, he made extensive use of the Internet for advertising and fundraising, and he was advised by James Carville.[20]

A candidate who polled unexpectedly well was 56-year-old anti-corruption parliamentarian Ramazan Bashardost, an ethnic Hazara. He ran a low-budget campaign was appealed to reform-minded Afghans outside his core Hazara base. However, Mohaqiq's backing (he was allied to Karzai at that time) apparently helped Karzai carry the Hazara heartland of Bamiyan province.

The Election Results

Taliban intimidation and voter apathy appear to have suppressed the total turnout to about 5.8 million votes cast, or about a 35% turnout, far lower than expected. Twenty-seven Afghans, mostly security forces personnel, were killed in election-day violence. Some observers said that turnout among women was primarily because there were not sufficient numbers of female poll workers to make women feel comfortable enough to vote. In general, however, election observers reported that poll workers were well trained, and the voting process was orderly.

Clouding the election substantially were the widespread fraud allegations coming from all sides. Dr. Abdullah held several news conferences after the election, purporting to show evidence of systematic election fraud by the Karzai camp. The ECC, in statements, stated its belief that there was substantial fraud likely committed, mostly by Karzai supporters. The final, uncertified total was released on September 16, 2009, and showed Karzai at 54.6% and Dr. Abdullah at 27.7%. Bashardost and Ghani received single-digit vote counts (9% and 3% respectively).

Vote Certified/Runoff Mandated

The constitution required that a second-round runoff, if needed, be held two weeks after the results of the first round are certified. Following the release of the vote count, the complaints evaluation period began which, upon completed, would yield a "certified" vote result. On September 8, 2009, the ECC ordered a recount of 10% of polling stations (accounting for as many as 25% total votes). Polling stations were considered "suspect" if the total number of votes exceeded the 600 maximum number allotted to each polling station; or where any candidate received 95% or more of the total valid votes cast at that station. Perhaps reflecting political sensitivities, the recount consisted of a sampling of actual votes.[21]

---

[20] Mulrine, Anna, "Afghan Presidential Candidate Takes a Page From Obama's Playbook," *U.S. News and World Report*, June 25, 2009.

[21] "Afghan Panel to Use Sampling in Recount," *USA Today*, September 22, 2009.

On October 20, 2009, the ECC determined, based on its investigation, that about 1 million Karzai votes, and about 200,000 Abdullah votes, were considered fraudulent and were deducted from their totals. The final, certified, results of the first round were as follows: Karzai—49.67% (according to the IEC; with a slightly lower total of about 48% according to the ECC determination); Abdullah—30.59%; Bashardost—10.46%; Ghani—2.94%; Yasini—1.03%; and lower figures for the remaining field.[22]

During October 16-20, 2009, U.S. and international officials, including visiting Senator John Kerry, met with Karzai to attempt to persuade him to acknowledge that his vote did not exceed the 50%+ threshold needed for a first-round victory. On October 21, 2009, the IEC accepted the ECC findings and Karzai conceded the need for a runoff election. A date was set as November 7, 2009. Abdullah initially accepted. In an attempt to produce a fair second round, UNAMA, which provided advice and assistance to the IEC, requested that about 200 district-level election commissioners be replaced and that there be fewer polling stations—about 5,800, compared to 6,200 previously—to eliminate polling stations where very few votes were expected to be cast.

Prior to the ECC vote certification, Dr. Abdullah told CRS at a meeting in Kabul on October 15, 2009, that he might be willing to negotiate with Karzai on a "Joint Program" of reforms—such as direct election of provincial governors—to avoid a runoff. However, some said the constitution does not provide for a negotiated settlement and that the runoff must proceed. Others said that a deal between the two, in which Abdullah dropped his candidacy, could have led the third-place finisher, Bashardost, to assert that he must face Karzai in a runoff. Still others say the issue could have necessitated resolution by Afghanistan's Supreme Court.

The various pre-runoff scenarios were mooted on November 1, 2009, when Dr. Abdullah refused to participate in the runoff on the grounds that problems that plagued the first round were unresolved. Some believe Abdullah pulled out because he believed he would not prevail in the second round. On November 2, 2009, the IEC issued a statement saying that, by consensus, the body had determined that Karzai, being the only candidate remaining in a two-person runoff, should be declared the winner. The Obama Administration accepted the outcome as "within Afghanistan's constitution," on the grounds that the fraud had been investigated. The United States, U.N. Secretary General Ban Ki Moon (visiting Kabul), and several governments, congratulated Karzai. Secretary of State Clinton praised Dr. Abdullah for his relatively moderate speech announcing his pullout. However, the marred elections process was a major factor in a September-November 2009 high-level U.S. strategy reevaluation because of the centrality of a credible, legitimate partner Afghan government to U.S. strategy.[23]

As noted above, the election for the provincial council members were not certified until December 29, 2009. The council members took office in February 2010.

September 18, 2010, Parliamentary Elections

The split over the conduct of the presidential elections widened in the run-up to the September 18, 2010, parliamentary elections. Mechanisms to prevent fraud were not fully implemented and the results continue to be disputed as of July 2011, largely paralyzing the institutional functioning of the Assembly and its role as a check and balance on the Karzai government. As a result, the

---

[22] See IEC website for final certified tallies, http://www.iec.org.af/results.

[23] Fidler, Stephen and John W. Miller, "U.S. Allies Await Afghan Review," *Wall Street Journal*, September 25, 2009.

political structure of Afghanistan has continued to fragment, even as the government assumers greater responsibility in the context of a transition to Afghan security leadership beginning in July 2011. The July 20, 2010, Kabul conference final communiqué included an Afghan government pledge to initiate, within six months, a strategy for long-term electoral reform.

Election Timing

On January 2, 2010, the IEC had initially set National Assembly elections for May 22, 2010. The IEC view was that this date was in line with a constitutional requirement for a new election to be held well prior to the expiry of the current Assembly's term. However, U.S., ECC, UNAMA, and officials of donor countries argued that Afghanistan's flawed institutions would not be able to hold free and fair elections under this timetable. Among the difficulties noted were that the IEC lacks sufficient staff, given that some were fired after the 2009 election; that the IEC lacks funds to hold the election under that timetable; that the U.S. military buildup will be consumed with securing still restive areas at election time; and that the ECC's term expired at the end of January 2010. A functioning ECC was needed to evaluate complaints against registered parliamentary candidates because there are provisions in the election law to invalidate the candidacies of those who have previously violated Afghan law or committed human rights abuses.

The international community pressed for a delay of all of these elections until August 2010 or, according to some donors, mid-2011.[24] Bowing to funding and the wide range of other considerations mentioned, on January 24, 2010, the IEC announced that the parliamentary elections would be postponed until September 18, 2010. Other experts said that the security issues, and the lack of faith in Afghanistan's election institutions, necessitated further postponement.[25]

About $120 million was budgeted by the IEC for the parliamentary elections, of which at least $50 million came from donor countries, giving donors leverage over when the election might take place. The remaining $70 million was funds left over from the 2009 elections. Donors had held back the needed funds, possibly in an effort to pressure the IEC to demonstrate that it is correcting the flaws identified in the various "after-action" reports on the 2009 election. With the compromises and Karzai announcements below, those funds were released as of April 2010.

Election Decree/Reform

With the dispute between the Karzai government and international donors continuing over how to ensure a free and fair election, in February 2010 Karzai signed an election decree that would supersede the 2005 election law and govern the 2010 parliamentary election.[26] The Afghan government argued that the decree supersedes the constitutional clause that any new election law not be adopted less than one year prior to the election to which that law will apply.

---

[24] Trofimov, Yaroslav, "West Urges Afghanistan to Delay Election," *Wall Street Journal*, December 11, 2009.

[25] Rondeaux, Candace, "Why Afghanistan's September Elections Ought to Be Postponed." *Washington Post*, July 11, 2010.

[26] Partlow, Joshua, "Afghanistan's Government Seeks More Control Over Elections," *Washington Post*, February 15, 2010.

Substantively, some of the provisions of the election decree—particularly the proposal to make the ECC an all-Afghan body—caused alarm in the international community. Another controversial element was the registration requirements of a financial deposit (equivalent of about $650), and that candidates obtain signatures of at least 1,000 voters. On March 14, 2010, after discussions with outgoing UNAMA head Kai Eide, Karzai reportedly agreed to cede to UNAMA two "international seats" on the ECC, rather than to insist that all five ECC members be Afghans. Still, the majority of the ECC seats were Afghans.

The election decree became an issue for Karzai opponents and others in the National Assembly who seek to assert parliamentary authority. On March 31, the *Wolesi Jirga* voted to reject the election decree. However, on April 3, 2010, the *Meshrano Jirga* decided not to act on the election decree, meaning that it was not rejected by the Assembly as a whole and governed the September 18, 2010, National Assembly elections. Karzai upheld his pledge to implement the March 2010 compromise with then UNAMA head Eide by allowing UNAMA to appoint two ECC members and to implement a requirement that at least one non-Afghan ECC member concur in decisions.

Among other steps to correct the mistakes of the 2009 election, the Afghan Interior Ministry planned instituted a national identity card system to curb voter registration fraud. However, observers say that registration fraud still occurred. On April 17, 2010, Karzai appointed a new IEC head, Fazel Ahmed Manawi, a Tajik, who drew praise from many factions (including "opposition leader" Dr. Abdullah, who is half Tajik and identifies with that ethnicity) for impartiality. The IEC also barred 6,000 poll workers who served in the 2009 election from working the 2010 election.

Preparations and the Vote

Preparations for the September 18 election proceeded without major disruption, according to the IEC. Candidates registered during April 20-May 6, 2010. A list of candidates was circulated on May 13, 2010, including 2,477 candidates for the 249 seats.[27] These figures included 226 candidates who registered but whose documentation was not totally in order; and appeal restored about 180 of them. On May 30, 2010, in a preliminary ruling, 85 other candidates were disqualified as members of illegal armed groups. However, appeals and negotiations restored all but 36 in this latter category. A final list of candidates, after all appeals and decisions on the various disqualifications, was issued June 22. The final list included 2,577 candidates, including 406 women. Sixty-two candidates were invalidated by the ECC, mostly because they did not resign their government positions, as required.

Voter registration was conducted June 12-August 12. According to the IEC, over 375,000 new voters were registered, and the number of eligible voters was about 11.3 million. Campaigning began June 23. Many candidates, particularly those who are women, said that security difficulties have prevented them from conducting active campaigning. At least three candidates and 13 candidate supporters were killed by insurgent violence.

On August 24, 2010, the IEC announced that the Afghan security forces say they would only be able to secure 5,897 of the planned 6,835 polling centers. To prevent so-called "ghost polling

---

[27] The seat allocation per province is the same as it was in the 2005 parliamentary election—33 seats up for election in Kabul; 17 in Herat province; 14 in Nangarhar, 11 each in Qandahar, Balkh, and Ghazni; 9 in Badakhshan, Konduz, and Faryab, 8 in Helmand, and 2 to 6 in the remaining provinces. Ten are reserved for Kuchis (nomads).

stations" (stations open but where no voters can go, thus allowing for ballot-stuffing), the 938 stations considered not secure were not opened. The IEC announcement stated that further security evaluation could lead to the closing of still more stations and, on election day, a total of 5,355 centers opened (304 of those slated to open did not, and for 157 centers there was no information available). In part to compensate, the IEC opened extra polling stations in centers in secure areas near to those that were closed.

On election day, about 5.6 million votes were cast out of about 17 million eligible voters. Turnout was therefore about 33%. A major issue suppressing turnout was security. At first, it appeared as though election-day violence was lower than in the 2009 presidential election. However, on September 24, NATO/ISAF announced that there were about 380 total attacks, about 100 more than in 2009. However, voting was generally orderly and the attacks did not derail the election.

Parliamentary Election Outcome

Preliminary results were announced on October 20, 2010, and final, IEC-certified results were to be announced by October 30, 2010, but were delayed until November 24, 2010, due to investigation of fraud complaints. While the information below illustrates that there was substantial fraud, the IEC and ECC have been widely praised by the international community for their handling of the fraud allegations.

Of the 5.6 million votes cast, the ECC invalidated 1.3 million (about 25%) after investigations of fraud complaints. The ECC prioritized complaints filed as follows: 2,142 as possibly affecting the election, 1,056 as unable to affect the result, and 600 where there will be no investigation. Causes for invalidation most often included ballot boxes in which all votes were for one candidate. About 1,100 election workers were questioned by ECC personnel, and 413 candidates were referred by the ECC to the Attorney General for having allegedly committed election fraud.

The results, as certified by the IEC, resulted in substantial controversy within Afghanistan and led to a political crisis. The certified results were as follows.

- About 60% of the lower house (148 out of 249) winners were new members.

- As noted above, Karzai's number of core supporters was reduced from about 90 to 60-70. This was in part because the number of Pashtuns elected was 94, down from 120 in the outgoing lower house. Several pro-Karzai candidates lost in Qandahar Province, and because many Pashtuns did not vote due to security reasons, in mixed Ghazni Province. The low Pashtun turnout in Ghazni caused Hazara candidates to win all 11 seats from the province, instead of 6 Pashtuns and 5 Hazaras in the outgoing lower house; this was a big factor in the reduction of the number of Pashtuns who won election. Several prominent pro-Karzai deputies were defeated, including Jamil Karzai, Pacha Khan Zadran, Mahmud Khan Suleimankhel (Paktika Province), and Muin Mirastyal (Konduz Province). The Hazara strength had no clear impact because many Hazaras support Karzai, although their increased political strength has caused ethnic tensions with the Pashtuns.

- Some observers note that some local militia commanders won election, adding to or replacing similar figures in past parliaments: the newly elected include Amanullah Guzar (Kabul) who may have been behind May 2006 rioting in Kabul against NGO offices; and Haji Abdul Zahir (Nangarhar), a member of the well-known "Eastern Shura" once headed by the assassinated Hajji Abdul Qadir and one-time Kabul Governor Hajji Din Mohammad. Other *mujahedin*-era figures were reelected, including Iqbal Safi (Kapisa), Zalmai Mujaddedi (Badakhshan), Fukkuri Beheshti (Bamiyan), and Shahzada Shahed (Kunar).

- Two ex-Taliban figures, Mullah Salam Rocketi, and Musa Wardak, were defeated.

- A date of the inauguration of the new parliament was set for January 20, 2011, at which time, under Afghan law, President Karzai would formally open the session.

Special Tribunal, Related Political Crisis, and Resolution

The certified results triggered a major political crisis, caused primarily by Pashtuns who felt they lost the election due to fraud. The issue brought the operations of the National Assembly to a virtual halt, with Karzai ruling by decree, with seven cabinet posts and a few Supreme Court seats remaining unfilled by permanent appointees, and, as discussed above, with certified election winners in the Assembly threatening to impeach him in July 2011.

Immediately after the election results were certified, Karzai took steps to address Pashtun grievances, but with its own interest in increasing the number of Pashtuns elected, in December 2010 the Karzai government (office of the Attorney General) indicted all seven IEC commissioners as well as the three Afghan members of the ECC. The deputy attorney general that same month urged election results to be voided and the Afghan Supreme Court to order a recount. There were weekly demonstrations against the fraud by about 300 candidates who felt deprived of victory, under a banner called the "Union of Afghan *Wolesi Jirga* Candidates 2010," led by defeated Ghazni candidate Daud Sultanzoy.

On December 28, 2010, at the instruction of the Supreme Court, Karzai issued a decree empowering a five-member tribunal to review fraud complaints. Many Afghans, including an independent watchdog group, "Free and Fair Election Foundation," maintained that the tribunal had no legal authority under the constitution to review the election. The IEC and ECC, backed by UNAMA and the international community, insisted that the certified results stand, asserting they are the only bodies under Afghan electoral law that have legitimate jurisdiction over election results. Still, on January 19, 2011, the day before the parliament was to convene, the tribunal leader, Judge Sediqullah Haqiq, announced it would need another month to evaluate the fraud allegations. On that basis, following the recommendation, the Karzai government postponed the inauguration of the new parliament by one month.

Defying Karzai and the special tribunal, about 213 of the certified winners met at the Intercontinental Hotel in Kabul on January 20, 2011, and reportedly decided to take their seats on Sunday, January 23, 2011, without Karzai's formal inauguration. Elected deputies at the meeting said they would try to convene at the parliament building but would meet elsewhere, if blocked. They elected an interim speaker, Hajji Mohammad Sarwar Osmani, from Farah Province. This would have rendered unclear the legal status of a self-convened parliament.

During January 20-25, 2011, with the lower house threatening to convene on its own, a compromise was found. Karzai agreed to inaugurate the lower house on January 26, 2011; that event took place. However, the ongoing fraud investigation by the special tribunal remained active, despite insistence by declared winners to terminate it. As noted, after its inauguration, the lower house elected a compromise candidate, Abdul Raouf Ibrahimi, from the Uzbek community, as speaker. This fell short of Karzai's goal of engineering selection of Sayyaf but accomplished his aim of denying Qanooni reselection to that post. The upper house was completed as of February 19, 2011, when Karzai made his 34 appointments.

The special tribunal process continued to investigate and to recount votes in several provinces. The crisis became acute on June 23, 2011, when the special tribunal ruled that 62 defeated candidates be reinstated. The National Assembly—containing the 62 people who would lose their seats if the tribunal's order were followed—subsequently passed a no-confidence vote against Attorney General Aloko. On August 10, 2011, Karzai appeared to defuse the eight month-long crisis; he issued a decree declaring that special court does not have jurisdiction to change election results, and that such changes are the role of the IEC. Subsequently, on August 21, 2011, the IEC implemented elements of a compromise urged by UNAMA by ruling that nine winners had won their seats through fraud and must be removed. This decision, with IEC chairman Manawi acknowledged was partly due to politics, removed fewer than the 17 that UNAMA had urged but more than the 5 the IEC reportedly thought would defuse the crisis. Some of the nine newly declared winners were sworn in on September 4, 2011, and the nine whose victories were overturned were barred from entering the parliament building. However, in protest of the decision, about 70 parliamentarians refused to convene and the Assembly was unable to obtain a quorum to act on legislation or government nominees, including Supreme Court vacancies. The boycotting parliamentarians ended their protest on October 8, 2011, paving the way for the National Assembly to resume full function.

2009 and 2010 Elections Alter Karzai-Assembly Relations

The exposure of widespread fraud in the 2009 and 2010 elections appeared to alienate Karzai from the National Assembly. In the confirmation process of his post-2009 election cabinet, National Assembly members, particularly the well-educated independents, objected to many of his nominees as "unknowns," as having minimal qualifications, or as loyal to faction leaders who backed Karzai in the 2009 election. Karzai's original list of 24 ministerial nominees (presented December 19) was generally praised by the United States for retaining the highly praised economic team (and most of that team was confirmed). However, overall, only 7 of the first 24 nominees were confirmed (January 2, 2010), and only 7 of the 17 replacement nominees were confirmed (January 16, 2010), after which the Assembly went into winter recess. Although then UNAMA head Kai Eide called the vetoing of many nominees a "setback" to Afghan governance, Pentagon Press Secretary Geoff Morrell said on January 6, 2010, that the vetoing by parliament reflected a "healthy give and take" among Afghanistan's branches of government. Another five (out of seven nominees) were confirmed on June 28, 2010, although one was a replacement for the ousted Interior Minister Atmar.

The differences over cabinet selections continued after the resolution in 2011 of the Assembly elections, although perhaps with less intensity, suggesting Karzai and the Assembly have sought to put aside differences and focus on governing. On March 12, 2012, the National Assembly confirmed most of those ministers who were serving in an acting capacity—including the controversial Ismail Khan—as well as some new nominees. As noted above, on September 16, 2012, the Assembly approved Karzai's nominees for heads of the three main security institutions.

Implications for the United States of the Afghan Elections Disputes

U.S. officials express clear U.S. neutrality in all Afghan elections. However, U.S. officials remained concerned that the 2009 and 2010 elections, and subsequent political crisis, would complicate the July 2011 start of the transition to Afghan security leadership, which began in seven areas (three provinces and four cities). 10,000 U.S. troops were withdrawn in late 2011 and an additional 23,000 will leave by September 2012. The election fraud and disputes have purportedly affected the perceptions of the Afghan people about the legitimacy of the Afghan government and its ability to take the lead on security by the end of 2014, according to current plans. The August 10, 2011, Karzai decree may serve to alleviate some of these concerns.

Afghans close to Karzai believe that the U.S. posture on the Afghan elections strained relations between the two countries. In the 2009 presidential election, Karzai reportedly believed the United States was hoping strong candidates might emerge to replace him. The United States repeatedly stated its neutrality in all Afghan elections, and Ambassador Timothy Carney headed the 2009 U.S. election support effort at U.S. Embassy Kabul, tasked to ensure that the United States was even-handed.

2014 Presidential Elections: Karzai Says He Will Leave Office, Looks for Successor

Under the constitution, the next presidential elections are to be held by the end of 2014. There is no clear frontrunner to succeed Karzai, although a number of candidates receive attention from observers, particularly those who ran before. Some observers say that, in the interests of unity approaching the 2014 security transition, factions should unify around a single successor who could be elected by acclamation. It is not clear whether that idea will resonate among major factions.

The potential Pashtun contenders are Ghul Agha Sherzai, Ashraf Ghani, former Interior Minister Ali Jalali (a Pashtun), Education Minister Faruq Wardak, and others. Some fear that Karzai may try to position himself to wield influence in a successor government by endorsing and working on behalf of one of these Pashtun candidates, and several of them are said to be seeking Karzai's backing. Karzai has said he does not want any of his brothers to run to succeed him, but Qayyum is said to be pondering a run, as is Mahmoud, despite the many allegations of his profiting from his brother's presidency. Ghani appeared to confirm his interest in a run in June 2012 by publicly criticizing corruption in government.

Of the Tajik representatives, those who might run include Dr. Abdullah, Ahmad Zia Masoud, and Amrollah Saleh. Dr. Abdullah is said to be encouraging Hanif Atmar, a Pashtun mentioned above, to run as his first vice president in an effort to appeal to Pashtuns. However, a run by him might conflict with a run by the other Tajiks, and it is likely these figures will try to unite behind one Tajik representative.

Parliamentarian Fawzia Koofi, mentioned above, has stated in editorials since late 2011 that she will run, although her gender as well as her Tajik ethnicity would lead most observers to conclude she is not favored to win. Ramazan Bashardost, a Hazara, is likely to again run on an anti-corruption platform.

Some Karzai critics have claimed he still plans to alter the constitution to allow himself to run for a third time, or possibly engineer a *loya jirga*—invoking national security grounds—to ask him to stay in office after 2014. At a June 15, 2011, Senate Appropriations Committee hearing, then Secretary of Defense Gates said Karzai had abandoned any such thinking and would leave office in 2014. Some U.S. officials sought to persuade Karzai to make a more public and definitive declaration to that effect. On August 12, 2011, the palace issued a statement that Karzai had told a group of parliamentarians that he would end his presidency after his second term. Press reports in September 2012 say that Karzai has been telling diplomats and others in Kabul that he might not endorse any candidate or involve himself in the 2014 election in any way—apparently trying to put to rest other assessments that Karzai wants to wield post-2014 political influence from behind the scenes. On the other hand, some read his reshuffling on September 20, 2012, of 10 of the 34 provincial governorships as an effort to place loyalists in position to support his favored candidate in the 2014 election.

Election Timing, Other Ongoing Electoral Issues

The international community is concerned about the 2014 election for its implications for Afghanistan's ability to govern beyond the 2014 transition. In April 2012, Karzai acknowledged that he had begun discussing with aides the possibility of advancing the election to some time in 2013. The public explanation for raising this possibility is that international troops will be leaving by the end of 2014, and more foreign troops will be available to secure the election in 2013 than in 2014. However, some might argue that moving the election up gives well-known Karzai associates a political advantage over lesser known figures. However, Karzai's July 26, 2012, administrative reform decree directs the IEC to prepare a plan for registering candidates in 2014, suggesting Karzai may have dropped consideration of moving the election forward.

The July 8, 2012, Tokyo donors' conference resulted in the "Tokyo Mutual Accountability Framework," which stipulated economic aid incentives for Afghanistan in return for demonstrating progress in governance and against corruption. One of the Framework's stipulations is that Afghanistan conduct "credible, inclusive and transparent Presidential and Parliamentary elections in 2014 and 2015," including to "develop, by early 2013, a comprehensive election timeline through 2015 for electoral preparations and polling dates." [28]

Currently, electoral mechanisms continue to function, but reform is uncertain. As noted above, in August 2011, Karzai recognized formally the primacy of the IEC in determining the outcome of an election. IEC Chairman Manawi continues until early 2013, as does the term of IEC commissioner Abdul Pashaye. On December 19, 2011, Karzai swore in five new commissioners he appointed, a move that renewed criticism of mechanisms and laws that allow the president to appoint election officials. That same month the IEC signed a two-year assistance program by UNDP called ELECT II (Legal and Electoral Capacity for Tomorrow). Still, the 2014 election will require a new election law setting the framework for the IEC and ECC composition, and that law has not been adopted by the National Assembly to date.

---

[28] http://www.embassyofafghanistan.org/article/the-tokyo-declaration-partnership-for-self-reliance-in-afghanistan-from-transition-to-transf

Afghan Governing Capacity and Performance[29]

Some believe that Afghanistan will revert to a terrorist haven unless effective governance is well established before the transition to Afghan leadership is completed by 2014. U.S. and U.N. reports assess that there has been progress in the capacity of Afghan institutions to provide services; however, the low baseline of Afghan capacity means significant work remains. Many of the shortcomings in governance are attributed to all of the political disputes, alleged corruption, and the lack of workers trained or skilled in governmental affairs that are discussed below.

In major Afghanistan policy addresses, President Obama has consistently stressed that more needed to be done to promote the legitimacy and effectiveness of the Afghan government at both the Kabul and local levels. In the latter statement, he said: "The days of providing a blank check [to the Afghan government] are over." The U.S.-Afghanistan Strategic Partnership Agreement, signed in Afghanistan on May 1, 2012, commits the United States (beyond 2014) to "support the Afghan government in strengthening the capacity, self-reliance, and effectiveness of Afghan institutions and their ability to deliver basic services." Of the FY2013 request for about $2.3 billion in economic aid to Afghanistan, nearly one-third of the request is for programs to help promote good governance, human rights, rule of law, political competition, and civil society.

Earlier, the Obama Administration developed about 45 different metrics to assess progress in building Afghan governance and security, as it was required to do (by September 23, 2009) under P.L. 111-32, an FY2009 supplemental appropriation.[30] UNAMA, headed in Kabul by Jan Kubis, also evaluates Afghan governance according to numerous metrics. Afghan progress according to these metrics is presented in reports of the Secretary-General to the U.N. General Assembly, such as a report released March 5, 2012 (U.N. document number: A/66/728-S/2012/133)

The Tokyo Framework of Mutual Accountability, cited above, issued at the conclusion of the July 8, 2012, Tokyo donors' conference, makes aid incentives for Afghanistan (portions of $16 billion pledged through 2015) conditional on several governance measures including:[31]

- The holding of credible, inclusive, and transparent elections in 2014 and 2015.

- Improved access to justice, and respect for human rights, particularly for women and children.

- Improved integrity of public financial management and the commercial banking sector.

- Improved revenue systems and budget execution.

In part to demonstrate that Afghanistan would uphold those commitments, the Karzai administrative reform decree issued July 26, 2012, requires virtually every ministry and

---

[29] Some information in this section is from the State Department report on human rights in Afghanistan for 2011, May 24, 2012.

[30] "Evaluating Progress in Afghanistan-Pakistan" Foreign Policy website, http://www.foreignpolicy.com/articles/2009/09/16/evaluating_progress_in_afghanistan_pakistan.

[31] http://www.embassyofafghanistan.org/article/the-tokyo-declaration-partnership-for-self-reliance-in-afghanistan-from-transition-to-transf

---

government body to develop a work plan, complete unfinished tasks, file specified reports, or carry out specified reforms.[32]

Expanding Central Government Capacity

The international community has had mixed success in shifting authority in Afghanistan from traditional leaders and relationships to transparent and effective state institutions. Afghan ministries have greatly increasing their staffs and technological capabilities (many ministry offices now have modern computers and communications, for example). Afghan-led governmental reform and institution-building programs under way, all with U.S. and other donor assistance, include training additional civil servants, instituting merit-based performance criteria, basing hiring on qualifications rather than kinship and ethnicity, and weeding out widespread governmental corruption.

However, the government still faces a relatively small recruitment pool of workers with sufficient skills and many are reluctant to serve in the provincial offices of the central government ministries, particularly in provinces where there is still substantial violence. U.S. mentors and advisers serve in virtually all the Afghan ministries. Afghanistan has also tried to address the problem of international donors luring away Afghan talent with higher salaries, by pledging at the July 20, 2010, Kabul conference to reach an understanding with donors, within six months, on a harmonized salary scale for donor-funded salaries of Afghan government personnel. Discussions have been held between the Afghan government and donors on this issue.

The Afghan Civil Service

The low level of Afghan bureaucratic capacity is being addressed in a number of ways, but slowly. There are about 500,000 Afghan government employees, although the majority of them are in the security forces. A large proportion of the remainder work as teachers. On several occasions, the United States has funded jobs fairs that have recruited some new civil servants.

To increase the proficiency of government, during late 2010-early 2011, the government instituted merit-based appointments for senior positions, such as deputy provincial governors and district governors, and converted those positions to civil servants rather than political appointees. However, that effort stalled in April-September 2011, according to the October 2011 DOD report, because Karzai has not yet approved merit-based selectees for 14 deputy governor positions. If approved, more than three-quarters of Afghanistan's 34 provinces would have merit-based deputy governors.

The key institution that is deciding on merit based appointments and standardizing job descriptions, salaries, bonuses, and benefits is the Afghan Independent Administrative Reform and Civil Service Commission (IARCSC). The commission has thus far redefined more than 80,000 civil servant job descriptions. The Afghan cabinet drafted a revised civil service law to institute merit-based hiring and give the IARCSC a legal underpinning; it was ratified by the National Assembly in late 2011 and replaced a less-specific September 2005 civil service law.

---

[32] Text of the decree "On the Execution of Content of the Historical Speech of June 21, 2012, in the Special Session of the National Assembly. Provided to CRS by the Embassy of Afghanistan in Washington, D.C. July 16, 2012.

Under a USAID program called the Civilian Technical Assistance Plan, the United States is providing technical assistance to Afghan ministries and to the IARCSC. From January 2010 until January 2011, USAID, under a February 2010 memorandum of understanding, gave $85 million to programs run by the commission to support the training and development of Afghan civil servants. One of the commission's subordinate organizations is the Afghan Civil Service Institute, which trained over 16,000 bureaucrats during 2010-2011, according to the DOD 1230 report, and which has instituted an internship program for 1,000 interns in national civil service jobs and 2,000 interns in provincial and district offices. On-going training for civil servants is provided by an arm of the Civil Service Institute called the National Training Directorate (NTD).

According to the November 2011 report from the office of the Special Representative for Afghanistan and Pakistan, Ambassador Marc Grossman, USAID programs are helping employees of the state-owned Afghan power company (DABS) to manage Afghanistan's power grid and bill its customers. USAID programs have also trained 250 Ministry of Mines personnel in geology to try to help develop Afghanistan's extractive industries sector.

Many Afghan civil service personnel undergo training in India, building on growing relations between Afghanistan and India. Japan and Singapore also are training Afghan civil servants on good governance, anti-corruption, and civil aviation. Singapore and Germany will, in 2011, jointly provide technical assistance in the field of civil aviation. Some of these programs are conducted in partnership with the German Federal Foreign Office and the Asia Foundation.

The Afghan Budget Process

The international efforts to build up the central government are reflected in the Afghan budget process. The Afghan government controls its own funds as well as those of directly supplied donor funds. The Afghan budget year follows the solar year, which begins on March 21 of each year, which also corresponds to the Persian New Year (*Nowruz*). In early February 2011, the National Assembly adopted a 2011 national budget (March 2011-March 2012) in line with its responsibilities. However, the lack of a quorum in the Assembly in mid- to late-2011 slowed consideration of a budget for 2012 (March 2012-March 2013), as did an initial voting down of the 2012 budget by the lower house of the National Assembly in March 2012.

The Afghan budget is a "unitary" (centralized) system. Once a budget is adopted by the full National Assembly (first the upper house and then the lower house, and then signed by Karzai), the funds are allocated to central government ministries and other central government entities. Some of the elected provincial councils, appointed provincial governors, and district governors formulate local budget requirements and help shape the national budget process, but no locality controls its own budget. These local organs do approve the disbursement of funds by the central entities (called *mustofiats*, accounting offices in each of Afghanistan's 34 provinces). The Tokyo Mutual Accountability Framework, cited above, includes as one of its benchmarks the formalization of a provincial budgeting process with more systematic provincial input into the relevant ministries that formulate the national budget.

All revenue is collected by central government entities which implement the local programs but, according to experts, contributes to the widespread observation that local officials sometimes seek to retain or divert locally collected revenues. There are several pilot programs in place, including the Provincial Budget Pilot Program (PBPP) to improve budgetary planning integration between the national and provincial levels. To date, four ministries and the IDLG say they have made sound progress on this program and several other ministries are to be included in it in 2012-2013.

Donor Involvement in the Afghan Budget

The Afghan government is expected to take in about $2 billion in total revenue for all of 2012. Lacking resources, about 90% of total Afghan government expenditures (operating budget and development budget) was provided by international donors during 2006-2010, according to a GAO study issued September 2011. Of the 90%, the United States provide 62% and other donors provided 28% of total expenditures.[33] In 2011, donor funds covered 57% of the Afghan government's $2.2 billion operating budget.[34]

Although still wary of misuse, the United States has been slowly accommodating Afghan demands that aid be channeled through the Afghan government. More than 40% of U.S. aid was channeled through the Afghan government during FY2011. This is close to the target figure of 50% that was endorsed at the July 20, 2010, Kabul conference, and up from 21% in FY2009, according to a June 8, 2011, staff report of the Senate Foreign Relations Committee (*Evaluating U.S. Foreign Assistance to Afghanistan*). Increased percentages are predicated on U.S. assessments of the ability of individual ministries to accurately and transparently administer donated funds. According to that Foreign Relations Committee staff report, 14 Afghan ministries have received USAID and State Department funds.

Karzai has repeatedly said that the low level of direct funding has stunted the growth of Afghan government capacity. Many international development experts concur that only through direct funding will the Afghan government be able to develop the capacity and eventually the transparency to govern and deliver services effectively. The Tokyo Framework, cited earlier, provides incentives for Afghanistan by raising the percentage of donor funds channeled through the Afghanistan Reconstruction Trust Fund in exchange for Afghan governance progress—that fund gives money directly to Afghan ministries and thus gives the Afghan government substantial discretion as compared to other donated funds that are spent directly on projects. The Karzai administrative decree of July 26, 2012, provides for Afghan institutions to begin taking over the roles of donor-run Provincial Reconstruction Teams (PRTs). Karzai has long criticized the PRTs as preventing the Afghan government from expanding its own responsibilities and capacity.

Expanding Local (Subnational) Governance

As U.S. concerns about corruption in the central government increased after 2007, U.S. and allied policy has increasingly emphasized building local or "subnational" governance. This accords with U.S. strategy in Afghanistan, which is to build institutions that can govern and secure areas cleared by U.S. and NATO forces and preventing Taliban reinfiltration. The U.S. shift in emphasis complements that of the Afghan government, which asserts that it has itself long sought to promote local governance in Afghanistan's political and economic development.

---

[33] Government Accountability Office. "Afghanistan's Donor Dependence." September 20, 2011.

[34] The operating budget is greater than the government revenue because the operating budget includes some donor funds.

U.S. and partner country officials, as well as observers, say that local governance, particularly at the provincial level, is improving and expanding, particularly in areas secured by the 2010 U.S. "troop surge." U.S. officials say that Afghans are increasingly forming local councils and building ties to appointed local leaders in these cleared and secured areas. However, the April 2012 DOD report on Afghanistan stability (p.71) says subnational bodies "remain unable to provide many basic government services." This could be, in part, a result of attempts by Kabul to centralize decision making—the localities have their own governing bodies but the central government ministries in the provincial capitals of each province—not the subnational bodies—actually implement national programs. Local officials often disagree with the Kabul ministry representatives on priorities or on implementation mechanisms.

The Independent Directorate for Local Governance (IDLG)

In terms of local governance institution-building, a key institution was empowered in August 2007 when Karzai placed the selection process for local leaders (provincial governors and below) in a new Independent Directorate for Local Governance (IDLG)—and out of the Interior Ministry. The IDLG was headed until early 2011 by Jelani Popal, a member of Karzai's Popolzai tribe and a close Karzai ally. Some international officials say that Popal packed local agencies with Karzai supporters, where they were able to arrange votes for Karzai in the August 2009 presidential elections. He was replaced by Abdul Khaliq Farahi, a former diplomat who was kidnapped in Peshawar, Pakistan, and held for nearly three years (2008-2011) allegedly by militants linked to Al Qaeda.

In terms of donor programming, the IDLG is the implementing partner of the U.N. Development Program in the Afghanistan Subnational Governance Program II (ASGP-II). It was funded with $83.6 million from the European Community, Italy, Switzerland, and Britain. Its main achievement has been to fund national technical assistance for the IDLG.

The IDLG is an implementing partner for the District Delivery Program (DDP), now operating in 32 of the 364 districts of Afghanistan. It is a program created to improve government presence and service delivery at the district level, and is funded by the United States, Britain, Denmark, and France. U.S. funding for the program was suspended in July 2011 pending accountability of expenditures and a request for the IDLG and Ministry of Finance to satisfy several conditions, and has not reactivated to date.[35]

Provincial Governors and Provincial Councils

Many believe that, even more than institutional expansion, the key to effective local governance is the appointment of competent and incorruptible governors in all 34 Afghan provinces. U.N., U.S., and other international studies and reports all point to the beneficial effects (reduction in narcotics trafficking, economic growth, lower violence) of some of the strong Afghan civilian appointments at the provincial level. Provincial governors are still political appointees selected mostly for loyalty to Karzai although, as noted above, progress is being made in implementing a merit-based appointment system for deputy provincial governors and district governors. The July 26, 2012, Karzai decree directs the IDLG to open deputy governorships to competition within two months. The decree also requires the IDLG to fill open positions in the provinces within six

---

[35] DOD report on Afghanistan stability, April 2012, p.73.

months, to address the many vacancies in the provinces, including in the ministry offices in each provincial capital. It also requires a review of the performance of provincial governors' performance in combating corruption and improving governance.

A key example of a successful gubernatorial appointment has been the March 2008 appointment of Gulab Mangal as Helmand governor. He is from Laghman Province (eastern Afghanistan) and drew immediate skepticism from the local tribes and power-brokers of the south who repeatedly have urged Karzai to replace him. But, he has drawn wide praise from the United States and the international community for taking effective action to convince farmers to grow crops other than poppy. His leadership accounts for the reduction of cultivation in Helmand that have been noted since 2009. Mangal has played a key role in convening tribal *shuras* and educating local leaders on the benefits of the U.S.-led offensive to remove Taliban insurgents from Marjah town and install new authorities there. A key Mangal ally, who has reportedly helped bring substantial stability to the Nawa district, is Abdul Manaf.

On September 20, 2012, acting subsequent to his July 2012 administrative decree, Karzai shuffled 10 out of the 34 provincial governors, asserting that those taken out of their positions had fallen short on improving governance or combating corruption. Mangal was one of those removed, causing consternation among some of the international donors who have raved about his performance in Helmand. He was replaced by the little-known Gen. Mohammad Naeem. Some of the ousted governors were assigned to different provinces. Other than Helmand, the nine provinces where governors were changed include Wardak, Kabul, Takhar, Faryab, Baghlan, Nimruz, Laghman, Lowgar, and Badghis.

Other governors, such as Ghul Agha Shirzai and Atta Mohammad Noor (discussed above) are considered effective, but have been criticized for exercising excessive independence of central authority. Many of the other governors are considered weak, ineffective, or corrupt.

Provincial Councils

One problem noted by governance experts is that the role of the elected provincial councils is unclear. The elections for the provincial councils in all 34 provinces were held on August 20, 2009, concurrent with the presidential elections. The previous provincial council elections were held concurrent with the parliamentary elections in September 2005. In most provinces, the provincial councils do not act as true local legislatures and are considered weak compared to the power and influence of the provincial governors.

Perhaps the most significant role the provincial councils play is in choosing the upper house of the National Assembly (*Meshrano Jirga*). In the absence of district councils (no elections held or scheduled), the provincial councils elected in 2009 have chosen two-thirds (68 seats) of the 102-seat body. Karzai appointed the remaining 34 seats in February 2011.

District-Level Governance

The April 2012 DOD report on Afghan stability says that there was "measured progress" over the past six months in developing effective district governance. District governors are appointed by the president, at the recommendation of the IDLG. However, only a small proportion (about 5%-10%) of all district governors have been appointed through the merit-based appointment system in which qualifications are assessed by the IARCSC (see above). In some districts of Helmand that had fallen under virtual Taliban control until the July 2009 U.S.-led offensives in the province, there were no district governors in place at all. Some of the district governors, including in Nawa and Now Zad district, returned after the U.S.-led expulsion of Taliban militants.

The difficulty plaguing the expansion of district governance, in addition to security issues, is lack of resources. Only slightly more than half of all district governors (there are 364 districts) have any staff or vehicles.

District Councils

Another problem in establishing district level governance has been the fact that no elections for district councils have been held due to boundary and logistical difficulties. In his November 19, 2009, inaugural speech, Karzai said the goal of the government is to hold these elections along with the 2010 parliamentary elections. However, that was not accomplished and no date for these elections has been set. As a result, there is no one authoritative district-level representative body, but rather a collection of groupings established by donor programs. According to the April 2012 DOD report on Afghan stability, the Afghan government has agreed in principle to a roadmap leading to a single district level body, a roadmap to be endorsed by September 2012, although not necessarily implying district elections could be held by then.

Municipal and Village Level Authority

As are district governors, mayors of large municipalities are appointed. There are about 42 mayors nationwide, many with deputy mayors. Karzai pledged in his November 2009 inaugural that "mayoral" elections would be held "for the purpose of better city management." However, no municipal elections have been held and none is scheduled.

As noted throughout, there has traditionally been village-level governance by groups of tribal elders and other notables. That structure remains, particularly in secure areas, while village councils have been absent or only sporadically active in areas where there is combat. As noted above, a U.S. official in southern Afghanistan, Henry Ensher, said in January 2011 that councils have been formed in areas where security has been established by the 2010 U.S. "troop surge."

The IDLG and the Ministry of Rural Rehabilitation and Development (MRRD), with advice from India and other donors, also are empowering localities to decide on development priorities. The MRRD has formed about 30,000 Community Development Councils (CDCs) nationwide to help suggest priorities, and these bodies are eventually to all be elected.

U.S. Local Governance Advisory Capacity

As a consequence of the March 2009 Obama Administration review, to help build local governing capacity, the Administration recruited about 500 U.S. civilian personnel from the State Department, USAID, the Department of Agriculture, and several other agencies—and many additional civilians from partner countries joined them—to advise Afghan ministries, and provincial and district administrations. That effort raised the number of U.S. civilians in Afghanistan to about 975 by early 2010 and to 1,330 by August 2011. Of these, nearly 400 serve outside Kabul, up from 67 in early 2009.

Although many U.S. civilian officials work outside Kabul, there are about 1,100 employees at the U.S. Embassy in Kabul, from 18 different U.S. government agencies. To accommodate the swelling ranks, in early November 2010 a $511 million contract was let to Caddell Construction to expand it, and two contracts of $20 million each were let to construct U.S. consulates in Herat and Mazar-e-Sharif. The consulate in Mazar-e-Sharif, however, is not in operation because of concerns about the security of the building where it was to be located.

The Administration also has instituted appointments of "Senior Civilian Representatives" (SCR),[36] who are counterparts to the military commanders of each NATO/ISAF regional command (there are currently five of them). Each Senior Civilian Representative has 10-30 personnel on his/her team. For example, the SCR for Regional Command South is based at Qandahar airfield and interacts closely with the military command of the southern sector. The SCR for Regional Command East (RC-E) is based at Bagram Airfield.

Reforming Afghan Governance: Curbing Corruption[37]

Partly because many Afghans view the central government as "predatory," many Afghans and international donors have questioned Karzai's leadership. NATO estimates that about $2.5 billion in total bribes are paid by Afghans each year. Reducing corruption in government is a major focus of the Tokyo Mutual Accountability Framework, cited above, which requires Afghanistan to "enact and enforce the legal framework for fighting corruption." Karzai himself has repeatedly acknowledged that corruption is a major problem in Afghanistan. In a June 21, 2012, speech, he called on his government to step up the fight against corruption, and fighting corruption is a cornerstone of Karzai's July 26, 2012, administrative decree. However, concerns about Karzai's leadership on this issue center on implementation and his apparent reluctance to prosecute officials for corruption—particularly those related to or aligned with him politically. This stands in contrast to his attempts to vigorously prosecute for corruption those politically opposed to him.

High Level Corruption, Nepotism, and Cronyism

At the upper levels of government, some observers have asserted that Karzai deliberately tolerates officials who are allegedly involved in illicit activity and supports their receipt of lucrative contracts from donor countries, in exchange for their political support. Karzai's brother, Mahmoud, as discussed above, has apparently grown wealthy through real estate and auto sales ventures in Qandahar and Kabul, purportedly by fostering the impression he can influence his brother. Some observers who have served in Afghanistan say that Karzai has appointed some provincial governors to "reward them" and that these appointments have gone on to "prey" economically on the populations of that province.

Another trend that has attracted notice among Afghans is that several high officials, despite very low official government salaries, have acquired ornate properties in west Kabul since 2002. They allegedly have appropriated to themselves private land, the ownership of which was unclear, for

---

[36] For more information, see U.S. Department of Defense. "Report on Progress Toward Security and Stability in Afghanistan," April 2011; http://www.defense.gov/news/1230_1231Report.pdf, pp. 19-20.

[37] For more information, particularly on Rule of Law programs, see CRS Report R41484, *Afghanistan: U.S. Rule of Law and Justice Sector Assistance*, by Liana Sun Wyler and Kenneth Katzman.

homes, and housing business ventures. Redressing this issue is discussed in the "rule of law" section below.

Lower-Level Corruption

Observers who follow the issue say that most of the governmental corruption takes place in the course of performing mundane governmental functions, such as government processing of official documents (e.g., passports, drivers' licenses), in which processing services routinely require bribes in exchange for action.[38] Other forms of corruption include Afghan security officials' selling U.S./internationally provided vehicles, fuel, and equipment to supplement their salaries. In other cases, local police or border officials may siphon off customs revenues or demand extra payments to help guard the U.S. or other militaries' equipment shipments. Other examples include security commanders placing "ghost employees" on official payrolls in order to pocket their salaries. Corruption is fed, in part, by the fact that government workers receive very low salaries (about $200 per month, as compared to the pay of typical contractors in Afghanistan that might pay as much as $6,500 per month). Many observers say there is a cultural dimension to the corruption—that it is commonly expected by relatives and friends that those Afghans who have achieved government positions will protect those relations with favors, appointments, and contracts.

Administration Views and Policy on Corruption

As noted throughout, there is a consensus within the Administration on the wide scope of the corruption in Afghan government and the deleterious effect the corruption has on government popularity and effectiveness. The Administration wrestled throughout 2010 with the degree to which to press an anti-corruption agenda with the Karzai government, but, in early 2011, the Administration reportedly decided to prioritize reducing low-level corruption instead of investigations of high-level allies of Karzai.[39] The latter investigations have sometimes come into conflict with other U.S. objectives by causing a Karzai backlash. In addition, such investigations may complicate efforts to obtain the cooperation of Afghans who can help stabilize areas of the country. Some of these Afghans are said to be paid by the CIA for information and other support, and the National Security Council reportedly issued guidance to U.S. agencies to review this issue.[40]

Yet, U.S. officials believe that anti-corruption efforts must be pursued because corruption is contributing to a souring of Western publics on the mission as well as causing some Afghans to embrace Taliban insurgents. General Petraeus, the former top U.S. and NATO commander in Afghanistan, said he made anti-corruption a top priority to support his counter-insurgency strategy. A key deputy, General H.R. McMaster, formed several DOD task forces to focus on anti-corruption (*Shafafiyat*, Task Force Spotlight, and Task Force 2010) from a U.S. military/counter-insurgency perspective. These task forces, in part, review U.S. contracting strategies to enhance Afghan capacity and reduce the potential for corruption. The Shafafiyat task force announced in February 2012 that had caused the restitution of $11.1 million, $25.4 million in fines, and $3.4

---

[38] Filkins, Dexter, "Bribes Corrode Afghan's Trust in Government," *New York Times*, January 2, 2009.

[39] Strobel, Warren and Marisa Taylor. "U.S. Won't Pursue Karzai Allies in Anti-Corruption Campaign." McClatchy Newspapers, January 6, 2011.

[40] Chandrasekaran, Rajiv. "A Subtler Take to Fight Afghan Corruption." *Washington Post*, September 13, 2010.

million in seizures from allegedly fraudulent contractors, and has debarred or suspended more than 125 American, Afghan, and international workers for alleged fraud.[41]

Anti-Corruption Initiatives

Obama Administration officials have credited Karzai with allowing the United States and other donors to help develop oversight bodies to curb corruption. However, the credit is tempered by the lack of Afghan government provision of resources or attention to building these bodies. These criticisms were amplified in an April 30, 2012, report by the Special Inspector General for Afghanistan Reconstruction (SIGAR). At the July 20, 2010, Kabul conference—following onto the January 28, 2010, London conference—the Afghan government finalized a National Anti-Corruption Strategy ("Azimi report") and committed to enacting 37 laws to curb corruption. Very few of these laws have been enacted, although the Afghan cabinet has drafted new anti-corruption and auditing laws and some regulations have been issued by Karzai decree.

- *Assets Declarations and Verifications.* During December 15-17, 2009, Karzai held a conference in Kabul to combat corruption. It debated requiring deputy ministers and others to declare their assets, not just those at the ministerial level. That requirement was imposed. Karzai himself declared his assets on March 27, 2009. The July 20, 2010, Kabul conference communiqué[42] included an Afghan pledge to verify and publish these declarations annually, beginning in 2010. According to a U.N. report of March 9, 2011, 1,995 senior Afghan officials had declared their assets. However, the SIGAR report of April 30, 2012, said that the government's progress for verification of the declarations continues to "fall short of U.S. expectations."

- *A Joint Monitoring and Evaluation Committee* to evaluate the government's performance in combating corruption was mandated by the Kabul conference communiqué to be established within three months of the conference (by October 2010). According to a June 23, 2011, U.N. report, the committee, supported by UNDP, was inaugurated on May 11, 2011. It was established by decree and is composed of three Karzai nominees and three international nominees.

- *High Office of Oversight.* In August 2008 Karzai, with reported Bush Administration prodding, set up the "High Office of Oversight for the Implementation of Anti-Corruption Strategy" (commonly referred to as the High Office of Oversight, HOO) with the power to identify and refer corruption cases to state prosecutors, and to catalogue the overseas assets of Afghan officials. It is headed by former IEC head Azizullah Ludin. On March 18, 2010, Karzai, as promised at the January 28, 2010, international meeting on Afghanistan in London, issued a decree giving the High Office direct power to investigate corruption cases rather than just refer them to other offices. However, the SIGAR reported on April 30, 2012, that the HOO's core functions either deteriorated or were ineffective during the first quarter of 2012. The July 26, 2012, Karzai administrative decree directs the HOO to, within six months, assess "private institutions' and government officials' suspicious wealth" and report those

---

[41] John Ryan. "Task Force Rooting Out Corruption in Afghanistan." *Army Times*, February 20, 2012.

[42] Communiqué text at http://www.nytimes.com/2010/07/21/world/asia/21kabultext.html.

findings to the president's office every two months. USAID is providing the HOO $30 million total during FY2011-FY2013 to build capacity at the central and provincial level. USAID pays for salaries of six HOO senior staff and provides some information technology systems as well.

- *Establishment of Additional Investigative Bodies: Major Crimes Task Force and Sensitive Investigations Unit.* Since 2008, several additional investigative bodies have been established under Ministry of Interior authority. The most prominent is the "Major Crimes Task Force," tasked with investigating public corruption, organized crime, and kidnapping. A headquarters for the MCTF was inaugurated on February 25, 2010, and it has been funded and mentored by the FBI, the DEA, the U.S. Marshal Service, Britain's Serious Crimes Organized Crime Agency, the Australian Federal Police, EUPOL (European police training unit in Afghanistan), and the U.S.-led training mission for Afghan forces. The MCTF has 169 investigators, according to U.S. officials.

  A related body is the Sensitive Investigations Unit (SIU), run by several dozen Afghan police officers, vetted and trained by the DEA.[43] This body led the arrest in August 2010 of a Karzai NSC aide, Mohammad Zia Salehi, on charges of soliciting a bribe from the New Ansari Money Exchange in exchange for ending a money-laundering investigation of the firm. The middle-of-the-night arrest prompted Karzai, by his own acknowledgment on August 22, 2010, to obtain Salehi's release and to say he would establish a commission to place the MCTF and SIU under more thorough Afghan government control. Following U.S. criticism that Karzai is protecting his aides (Salehi reportedly was involved in bringing Taliban figures to Afghanistan for conflict settlement talks), Karzai pledged to visiting Senate Foreign Relations Committee Chairman John Kerry on August 20, 2010, that the MCTF and SIU would be allowed to perform their work without political interference. In November 2010, the Attorney General's office said it had ended the prosecution of Salehi.

- *Anti-Corruption Unit, and an Anti-Corruption Tribunal.* These investigative and prosecution bodies were established by decree in 2009. Eleven judges have been appointed to the tribunal. The tribunal, under the jurisdiction of the Supreme Court, tries cases referred by an Anti-Corruption Unit of the Afghan Attorney General's office. However, of the approximately 2,000 cases investigated by the Anti-Corruption Unit, only 28 officials have been convicted to date. The Department of Justice suspended its training program for the Anti-Corruption Unit in early 2012 because of the unit's "lack of seriousness," according to the SIGAR report of April 30, 2012. One of the laws pledged during the July 20, 2010, Kabul conference would be enacted (by July 20, 2011) included one to legally empower the Anti-Corruption Tribunal and the Major Crimes Task Force. That has not been enacted by the National Assembly to date.

- *Prosecutions and Investigations of High-Level Officials.* The Afghanistan Attorney General's office has investigated at least 20 senior officials. The April 30, 2012, SIGAR report said there had been no progress by the Attorney General in undertaking new prosecutions in early 2012. Perhaps to address that criticism,

---

[43] Nordland, Ron and Mark Mazzetti. "Graft Dispute in Afghanistan Is Test for U.S." *New York Times*, August 24, 2010.

new investigations were announced in mid-2012. One such case is that of Minister of Mines Wahidullah Shahrani, although observers believe his opponents are actually trying to combat a draft mining law that some see as too favorable to foreign firms. Accusations in July 2012 against Finance Minister Omar Zakhiwal appear focused on corruption rather than policy issues: Afghan media used his bank statements to show unusual payments from outside organizations. HOO director Ludin has called on Zakhiwal to step down while the investigation unfolds. Karzai has not publicly defended Zakhiwal against the accusations. Some of those investigated previously included Commerce Minister Amin Farhang (for allegedly submitting inflated invoices for reimbursement); former Minister of Mines Mohammad Ibrahim Adel (who reportedly accepted a $30 million bribe to award a key mining project in Lowgar Province to China);[44] and former Minister of the Hajj Mohammad Siddiq Chakari (for accepting bribes to steer Hajj-related travel business to certain foreign tourist agencies). Chakari fled to Britain. Then Deputy Kabul Mayor Wahibuddin Sadat was arrested at Kabul airport in December 2009 for alleged misuse of authority.

- *EITI.* Relatedly, Afghanistan has signed up as a candidate to the Extractive Industries Transparency Initiative (EITI) which is intended to ensure that contracting for Afghanistan's mineral resources is free of corruption. Afghanistan hopes to become fully EITI compliant by April 2012. The World Bank gave Afghanistan a three year grant of $52 million to manage its natural resources effectively.

- *Salary Levels.* The government has tried to raise salaries, particularly of security forces, in order to reduce their inclination to solicit bribes. In November 2009, the Afghan government announced an increase in police salaries (from $180 per month to $240 per month). During his term as Interior Minister, Bismillah Khan was credited by DOD with instituting transparency and accountability in promotions and assignments.

- *Bulk Cash Transfers Out of Afghanistan.* At the July 2010 Kabul conference, the government pledged to adopt regulations and implement within one year policies to govern the bulk transfers of cash outside the country. This was intended to grapple with issues raised by reports, discussed below, of officials taking large amounts of cash out of Afghanistan (an estimated $4.5 billion taken out in 2011). U.S. officials say that large movements of cash are inevitable in Afghanistan because only about 5% of the population use banks and 90% use informal cash transfers ("hawala" system). The late Ambassador Holbrooke testified on July 28, 2010 (cited earlier), that the Afghan Central Bank has begun trying to control hawala transfers; 475 hawalas have been licensed, to date, whereas none were licensed as recently as 2009. In June 2010, U.S. and Afghan officials announced establishment of a joint task force to monitor the flow of money out of Afghanistan, including monitoring the flow of cash out of Kabul International Airport. On August 21, 2010, it was reported that Afghan and U.S. authorities would implement a plan to install U.S.-made currency counters at Kabul airport to track how officials had obtained their cash (and ensure it did not come from

---

[44] Partlow, Joshua, "Afghanistan Investigating 5 Current and Former Cabinet Members," *Washington Post*, November 24, 2009.

donor aid funds).[45] During 2011, the United States tripled the number of Homeland Security personnel devoted to training Afghan customs and border employees to curb bulk transfers and smuggling. On March 19, 2012, Central Bank Governor Noorullah Delawari said the Bank had imposed a $20,000 per person limit on cash transfers out of the country.

- *Auditing Capabilities.* The SIGAR has previously assessed that the mandate of Afghanistan's Control and Audit Office is too narrow and lacks the independence needed to serve as an effective watch over the use of Afghan government funds.[46] At the Kabul conference, the government pledged to submit to parliament an Audit Law within six months, to strengthen the independence of the Control and Audit Office, and to authorize more auditing by the Ministry of Finance. The government drafted an audit law but, according to the April 30, 2012, SIGAR report, the National Assembly's legislative committee rejected the draft law in early 2012.

- *Legal Review.* The Kabul conference communiqué committed the government to establish a legal review committee, within six months, to review Afghan laws for compliance with the U.N. Convention Against Corruption. Afghanistan ratified the convention in August 2008.

- *Local Anti-Corruption Bodies.* Some Afghans have taken it upon themselves to oppose corruption at the local level. Volunteer local inspectors, sponsored originally by Integrity Watch Afghanistan, are reported to monitor and report on the quality of donor-funded, contractor implemented construction projects. However, these local "watchdog" groups do not have an official mandate, and therefore their authority and ability to rectify inadequacies are limited.

Kabul Bank Scandal and Continuing Difficulties

The near-collapse of Kabul Bank is a prime example of how well-connected Afghans have avoided regulations and other restrictions in order to garner personal profit. Mahmoud Karzai is a major (7%+) shareholder in the large Kabul Bank, which is used to pay Afghan civil servants and police, and he reportedly received large loans from the bank to buy his position in it. Another big shareholder was Abdul Hussain Fahim, the brother of First Vice President Fahim and partner of Mahmoud Karzai on other ventures. The insider relationships were exposed in August and September 2010 when Kabul Bank reported large losses ($500 million initially) primarily from shareholder investments in Dubai properties, prompting President Karzai to appoint a Central Bank official to run the Kabul Bank. However, the government moves did not prevent large numbers of depositors from withdrawing their money from it.

In response to the crisis, the United States and other donors refused to recapitalize the bank, but it offered to finance an audit of Afghan banks, including Kabul Bank. The Finance Ministry decided instead in November 2010 to hire its own auditor—a move that suggested to some that high Afghan officials seek to avoid sharing the results with international donors. The International Monetary Fund (IMF) suspended its credit program for the Afghan government in November 2010 because of the scandal and demanded the entire Afghan banking industry undergo an

---

[45] Miller, Greg and Joshua Partlow. "Afghans, U.S. Aim to Plug Cash Drain." *Washington Post*, August 21, 2010.

[46] Madhani, Aamer. "U.S. Reviews Afghan Watchdog Authority." *USA Today*, May 12, 2010.

outside forensic audit and that those responsible be held accountable. That caused the holding up of $70 million World Bank/Afghan Reconstruction Fund (ARTF) in donor funds due to be paid June 11, 2011. Other donors suspended as much as $1.8 billion in economic aid because of the IMF suspension.

Amid Afghan confirmation that the questionable loans of the bank total over $925 million (including interest due), the IMF—as a condition of resuming its credit program—subsequently pushed for the bank to be sold. The Central Bank instead agreed to separate the bank's performing from non-performing assets and then dissolve or restructure the bank.[47] A version of the plan, which was subject to approval by an Afghan government committee, was formally approved and announced on April 21, 2011.

The "good bank" (part of the bank with deposits and which still functions) was financed by a Central Bank loan of $825 million. The Afghan Finance Ministry has promised to pay back the loan with recovered assets and tax revenues. On October 16, 2011, the National Assembly voted on a supplemental budget that enabled the Finance Ministry to reimburse the Central Bank loan over eight years. However, Assembly rejection of the 2012 budget in March 2012 held up an $80 million annual increment for this purpose.

The Afghan government, through its "Financial Dispute Resolution Commission," continues to try to recoup the lost funds. Of the estimated $925 million in losses, about $300 million of the losses are judged by the Afghans as untraceable because of a lack of documentation. As of mid-2012, the commission has recovered $128 million in cash and $145 million in property, mostly luxury villas in Dubai.[48] Central Bank governor Noorullah Delawari said in April 2012 that the country plans to sell Kabul Bank in June 2012; that has not occurred to date. Mahmoud Karzai and Fahim have reportedly repaid their loans from the Bank. The Tokyo Mutual Accountability Framework, discussed above, requires Afghanistan to continue asset recovery and to strengthen banking supervision though the Central Bank (Da Afghanistan Bank).

Attempting Accountability

The political fallout also produced some resolution. On January 15, 2011, the office of Afghan Attorney General Ishaq Aloko announced an investigation into what led to the near-collapse of the bank and the principals involved. The investigating commission briefed reporters on its findings on May 30, 2011, placing much of the blame on lax controls by the Central Bank and its governor, Abdul Qadir Fitrat. The government commission also largely absolved Mahmoud Karzai of any wrongdoing, saying he had paid off his loans, and naming other key figures, such as Dostam, as taking out $100,000 in unsecured loans. The following day, Central Bank governor Fitrat disputed the commission's conclusions. He had previously told parliament that Mahmoud Karzai owed $22 million. In part because of his feuding with figures such as Mahmoud Karzai, Fitrat fled Afghanistan for the United States and announced his resignation on June 27, 2011. Karzai subsequently barred U.S. advisers from the Central Bank. On December 11, 2011, Karzai called for the United States to extradite Fitrat to Afghanistan and blamed U.S. officials for knowing of the Bank's problems at an early stage but failing to alert Afghan authorities.

---

[47] Ernesto Londono. "Afghan Officials Opt to Dissolve Bank Draped in Scandal." *Washington Post*, March 27, 2011.

[48] Joshua Partlow. "Afghan Bureaucrat Tasked With Recovering Millions in Bad Loans." Washington Post, July 7, 2012. Afghanistan Plans to Sell Scandal-Scarred Kabul Bank in June. Bloomberg.com, April 11, 2012.

In a step toward holding principals accountable, on June 30, 2011, the government announced the arrest of two former Kabul Bank executives, Sherkhan Farnood and Khalilullah Frouzi, who allegedly allowed the concessionary loans to the high-level Afghans and their relatives. However, by late 2011, the detentions of the two had been relaxed and they were frequently sighted at various public places in Kabul.[49] On August 1, 2011, the Attorney General's office sent the names of about 15 people allegedly responsible for the scandal to Afghan courts for trial. On April 3, 2012, Karzai ordered a special prosecutor appointed and a special tribunal created to try those involved in the scandal. On June 2, 2012, at the urging of Karzai's office, 21 people were indicted by the special tribunal, including Farnood, Frouzi, Fitrat, nine other government officials, and nine other bank employees who were allegedly in positions to have known of and reported the fraud while it was occurring but did not.

The investigations, the recovery of some lost funds, and the start of a forensic audit of the bank suggested Afghanistan was moving to meet the IMF conditions for the restart of its credit program. On October 6, 2011, the IMF issued a statement that it would restore its credit program because of the investigations and because of the Afghan efforts to recover some of the Bank's funds. In November 2011, the IMF resumed its program by approving a $133 million loan to Afghanistan. That move restored the flow of some previously blocked donor funds, including U.S. contributions to the World Bank-run Afghanistan Reconstruction Trust Fund (ARTF).

The IMF also wants a timetable for another bank found by the Central Bank to be vulnerable to collapse, Azizi Bank, to shore up its finances. Another Afghan entity suspected of corruption is the New Ansari Money Exchange, a large money-trading operation. On February 18, 2011, the Treasury Department designated the New Ansari, and persons affiliated with it, as major money laundering entities under the "Kingpin Act," a designation that bans U.S. transactions with the designees. The Treasury Department accused the New Ansari and affiliates of serving as a vehicle for narcotics trafficking organizations.

Moves to Penalize Lack of Progress on Corruption

Several of the required U.S. "metrics" of progress, cited above, involve Afghan progress against corruption. A FY2009 supplemental appropriation (P.L. 111-32) mandated the withholding of 10% of about $90 million in State Department counter-narcotics funding subject to a certification that the Afghan government is acting against officials who are corrupt or committing gross human rights violations. In the 111th Congress, in June 2010, the Foreign Operations Subcommittee of the House Appropriations Committee deferred consideration of some of the nearly $4 billion in civilian aid to Afghanistan requested for FY2011, pending the outcome of a committee investigation of the issue. The subcommittee's action came amid reports that as much as $3 billion in funds have been allegedly embezzled by Afghan officials over the past several years.[50] In part on the basis of the findings of the House Appropriations Committee investigation, the Senate Appropriations Committee's FY2011 omnibus appropriation marked up in December 2010 required Administration certifications of progress against corruption as a condition of providing aid to Afghanistan. Some of this conditionality was included in the FY2011 continuing appropriations (P.L. 112-10). Aid conditionality based on Afghan performance against corruption,

---

[49] Matthew Rosenberg and Graham Bowley. "Intractable Afghan Graft Hampering U.S. Strategy." *New York Times*, March 8, 2012.

[50] Rosenberg, Matthew. "Corruption Suspected in Airlift of Billions in Cash From Kabul." *Wall Street Journal*, June 28, 2010.

on incorporation of women in the reconciliation process, and on reports on progress on the Kabul Bank scandal, are included in the FY2012 Consolidated Appropriation (P.L. 112-74). No U.S. funding for Afghanistan has been permanently withheld because of this or any other legislative certification requirement.

Rule of Law Efforts

U.S. efforts to curb corruption go hand-in-hand with efforts to promote rule of law. As of July 2010, the U.S. Embassy has an Ambassador rank official heading a "Rule of Law Directorate." U.S. funding supports training and mentoring for Afghan justice officials, direct assistance to the Afghan government to expand efforts on judicial security, legal aid and public defense, gender justice and awareness, and expansion of justice in the provinces. According to the SRAP report of November 2011, USAID's "Rule of Law Stabilization Program" had, as of then, trained 670 Afghan judges, over half the total in the country. The program also had expanded the Afghan Supreme Court's training program for new judges, and supports linkage between the traditional justice sector and the formal justice system. Some observers say that Afghanistan's counter-narcotics courts have demonstrated particular progress in achieving a steady stream of convictions of drug traffickers.

At the July 20, 2010, Kabul conference, the Afghan government committed to:

- Enact its draft Criminal Procedure Code into law within six months. This is one of the 37 laws pledged at the Kabul Conference would be enacted, but it has not been accomplished, to date.

- Improve legal aid services within the next 12 months. A December 10, 2010, U.N. report said that the Ministry of Justice had opened legal aid offices in some provinces. The Tokyo Framework, cited earlier, requires Afghanistan to "improve access to justice for all," suggesting that implementation has been weak.

- Strengthen judicial capabilities to facilitate the return of illegally seized lands. This commitment was made partly to address the issue discussed above in which powerful individuals have appropriated land for their homes and projects. USAID provided $56 million during FY2005-2009 to facilitate property registration. An additional $140 million is being provided from FY2010-2014 to inform citizens of land processes and procedures, and to establish a legal and regulatory framework for land administration.

- Align strategy toward the informal justice sector (discussed below) with the National Justice Sector Strategy.

Despite the international focus on the formal justice sector, some estimates say that 80% of cases are decided in the informal justice system. Many Afghans view the formal sector as riddled with corruption and unfairness, and continue to use local, informal mechanisms (*shuras, jirgas*) to adjudicate disputes—particularly with cases involving local property, familial or local disputes, or personal status issues In the informal sector, Afghans can usually expect traditional practices of dispute resolution to prevail, including the traditional Pashtun code of conduct known as *Pashtunwali.* Some of these customs, including traditional forms of apology ("*nanawati*" and "*shamana*") and compensation for wrongs done, are discussed at http://www.khyber.org/articles/2004/JirgaRestorativeJustice.shtml.

However, the informal justice system is dominated almost exclusively by males. For example, some disputes are resolved by families' offering to make young girls available to marry older men from the family that is the counter-party to the dispute, resulting in numerous forced marriages and child marriages. This practice is known as *baad*.

Some informal justice *shuras* take place in Taliban-controlled territory, and some Afghans may prefer Taliban-run *shuras* when doing so means they will be judged by members of their own tribe or tribal confederation.

One concern is how deeply the international community should become involved in the informal justice sector. U.S. programs have focused primarily on the formal justice system, but there has been increasing attention to the informal system because its use is so prevalent. USAID has implemented a pilot program to assist local *shuras* in four districts to establish a system to transmit their judicial rulings, in writing, to the district government. The rule of law issue is discussed in substantially greater depth in CRS Report R41484, *Afghanistan: U.S. Rule of Law and Justice Sector Assistance*, by Liana Sun Wyler and Kenneth Katzman.

Promoting Human Rights and Civil Society[51]

Since 2001, U.S. policy has been to build capacity in human rights institutions in Afghanistan and to promote civil society and political participation. As do previous years' State Department human rights reports, the report on Afghanistan for 2011 attributed the many human rights deficiencies observed primarily to overall lack of security, loose control over the actions of Afghan security forces, pervasive corruption, and societal discrimination particularly against women. A Human Rights Watch statement issued on the eve of the December 5, 2011, Bonn Conference was highly critical, saying that "ten years later [after the first Bonn Conference setting a transition from the Taliban era], many basic rights are still ignored or downplayed. While there have been improvements, the rights situation is still dominated by poor governance, lack of rule of law, impunity for militias and police, laws and policies that harm women, and conflict-related abuses."

On the other hand, there has been a significant proliferation of organizations that demand transparency about human rights deficiencies. Prominent examples of Afghan NGO's that monitor and agitate for improved human rights practices include the Afghanistan Human Rights and Democracy Organization, and the Research Institute for Women, Peace and Security. The December 5, 2011, Bonn Conference was preceded by meetings (December 2-3, 2011, in Bonn) of Afghan civil society activists, intended to help assess the progress of Afghan governance and highlight the role of civil society in governance. It is in part the work of these groups that has produced responses by the government. For example, Afghanistan's National Directorate of Security (intelligence directorate but with arrest powers), which has widely been accused of detainee abuse and torture, established in late 2011 a "human rights unit" to investigate these allegations. On June 2, 2012, Karzai ordered disarmed a local security unit whose members were accused of raping an 18-year old woman in Konduz Province. On July 9, 2012, Afghan forces were sent to track down Taliban militants who had executed a woman for adultery in Parwan Province.

---

[51] Information in this section is primarily from Department of State. 2011 Human Rights Report: Afghanistan, May 24, 2012; http://www.state.gov/j/drl/rls/hrrpt/humanrightsreport/index.htm?dynamic_load_id=186457#wrapper.

Institution-Building: The Afghanistan Independent Human Rights Commission (AIHRC)

One of the institutional human rights developments since the fall of the Taliban has been the establishment of the Afghanistan Independent Human Rights Commission (AIHRC). It is headed by a woman, Sima Simar, a Hazara Shiite from Ghazni Province. It acts as an oversight body over alleged human rights abuses but its members are appointed by the government and some believe it is not as aggressive or independent as some had hoped. However, its members are appointed by the president and, as an indication of government interference, in December 2011, Karzai dismissed its deputy chairman Ahmad Nader Nadery for his outspoken writings alleging abuses by traditional allies of Karzai. Nadery heads another civil society watchdog organization, the Free and Fair Election Foundation of Afghanistan, which was highly critical of Karzai and his allies for the 2009 and 2010 election fraud.

The July 20, 2010, Kabul conference communiqué contained a pledge by the Afghan government to begin discussions with the AIHRC, within six months, to stabilize its budgetary status. It pledged to provide $1 million per year, but has provided only half that amount. A December 10, 2010, U.N. Secretary General report says the Afghan cabinet has approved inserting a line item in the annual Afghan budget for the AIHRC, but the March 5, 2012, report of the Secretary General said the National Assembly has not regularized the AIHRC status within the national budget framework. USAID has given the AIHRC about $10 million per year since the fall of the Taliban.

Religious Influence on Society: National Ulema Council

Counterbalancing the influence of post-Taliban modern institutions such as the AIHRC are traditional bodies such as the National Ulema Council. The Council consists of the 150 most respected and widely followed clerics throughout Afghanistan, but it represents a network of about 3,000 clerics nationwide. It has increasingly taken conservative positions to limit free expression and social freedoms, such as the type of television and other media programs available on private media outlets.

In August 2010, 350 clerics linked to the Council voted to demand that Islamic law (Sharia) be implemented (including such punishments as stoning, amputations, and lashings) in order to better prevent crime. The government did not implement the recommendation, which would require amending the Afghan constitution, which does not implement Sharia. The Council's March 2, 2012, backing of Sharia interpretations of the rights of women is discussed below in the section on women's rights.

The government (Ministry of Hajj and Religious Affairs) is also involved in regulating religious practices. Of Afghanistan's approximately 125,000 mosques, 6,000 are registered and funded by the government. Clerics in these mosques are paid about $100 per month and, in return, are expected to promote the government line. In April 2012, the Ministry decreed that it would fire government-funded clerics who refuse to heed warnings and preach violence or incitement.

Riots over Quran Burnings and Anti-Islamic Video: 2011 and 2012

As an illustration of Afghanistan's Islamic conservatism, riots have broken out in two successive years over what some Afghans perceived as U.S. disrespect of Islam. On April 2, 2011, hundreds of Afghans rioted in the normally quiet (and non-Pashtun) city of Mazar-e-Sharif to protest the burning of a Quran by a Florida pastor a few weeks earlier. The rioters, who had been instigated by the sermons of three mullahs (Islamic preachers) at the city's signature Blue Mosque, stormed the U.N. compound in the city and killed at least 12 people, including 7 U.N workers. Over the next several days, similar, but less violent, demonstrations took place in Qandahar and other Afghan cities until sentiment calmed. Earlier, in September 2010, some National Ulema Council figures organized protests against plans by the Florida pastor to burn Qurans, although that burning was not conducted following international and U.S. criticism of the pastor.

A more serious eruption occurred in late February 2012 over the mistaken U.S. discarding of Qurans used by detainees at Bagram Airfield. Riots and protests occurred in several cities, including the normally peaceful and pro-U.S. north. The public reaction to the Quran burning was more intense than it was following the March 11, 2012, killing of 16 Afghans allegedly by a U.S. soldier, Robert Bales, who is in U.S. military custody.

On September 17, 2012, several hundred Afghans rioted outside a U.S. training facility east of Kabul city to protest a video produced in the United States ("Innocence of Muslims") that mocks the Prophet Muhammad. Afghan police protected the facility from assault from the crowd.

These perceived U.S. slights may account for some of the killings of U.S. military personnel by Afghan security forces over the past few years. The so-called "green on blue" attacks have caused tensions between Afghan forces and their U.S. mentors, and prompted U.S. commanders to impose counter-measures that potentially complicate the U.S. effort to accelerate the transition to Afghan security before the end of 2014.

Religious Freedom

The July-December 2010 International Religious Freedom report (released September 13, 2011)[52] says that respect for religious freedom declined throughout the reporting period, particularly for Christian groups and individuals. Members of minority religions, including Christians, Sikhs, Hindus, and Baha'i's, often face discrimination; the Supreme Court declared the Baha'i faith to be a form of blasphemy in May 2007. Northeastern provinces have a substantial population of Islamailis, a Shiite Muslim sect often called "Seveners" (believers in the Seventh Imam as the true Imam). Many Ismailis follow the Agha Khan IV (Prince Qarim al-Husseini), who chairs the large Agha Khan Foundation that has invested heavily in Afghanistan.

One major case that drew international criticism was a January 2008 death sentence, imposed in a quick trial, against 23-year-old journalist Sayed Kambaksh for allegedly distributing material critical of Islam. On October 21, 2008, a Kabul appeals court changed his sentence to 20 years in prison, a judgment upheld by another court in March 2009. He was pardoned by Karzai and released on September 7, 2009.

A positive development is that Afghanistan's Shiite minority, mostly from the Hazara tribes of central Afghanistan (Bamiyan and Dai Kundi provinces) can celebrate their holidays openly, a development unknown before the fall of the Taliban. Some Afghan Shiites follow Iran's clerical leaders politically, but Afghan Shiites tend to be less religious and more socially open than their co-religionists in Iran. The Hazaras are also advancing themselves socially and politically through

---

[52] http://www.state.gov/g/drl/rls/irf/2010_5/168240 htm.

education in such fields as information technology.[53] The former Minister of Justice, Sarwar Danesh, is a Hazara Shiite, the first of that community to hold that post. He studied in Qom, Iran, a center of Shiite theology. (Danesh was voted down by the parliament for reappointment on January 2, 2010, and again on June 28 when nominated for Minister of Higher Education.) The justice minister who was approved on January 16, 2010, Habibullah Ghalib, is part of Dr. Abdullah's faction, but not a Shiite Muslim. Ghaleb previously (2006) was not approved by the *Wolesi Jirga* for a spot on the Supreme Court. There was unrest among some Shiite leaders in late May 2009 when they learned that the Afghan government had dumped 2,000 Iranian-supplied religious texts into a river when an Afghan official complained that the books insulted the Sunni majority.

Several conversion cases have earned international attention. An Afghan man, Abd al-Rahman, who had converted to Christianity 16 years ago while working for a Christian aid group in Pakistan, was imprisoned and faced a potential death penalty trial for apostasy—his refusal to convert back to Islam. Facing international pressure, Karzai prevailed on Kabul court authorities to release him (March 29, 2006). His release came the same day the House passed H.Res. 736 calling on protections for Afghan converts. In May 2010, the Afghan government suspended the operations of two Christian-affiliated international relief groups claiming the groups were attempting to promote Christianity among Afghans—an assertion denied by the groups (Church World Service and Norwegian Church Aid). Another case arose in May 2010, when an amputee, Said Musa, was imprisoned for converting to Christianity from Islam, an offense under Afghan law that leaves it open for Afghan courts to apply a death sentence under Islamic law (Shariah). The arrest came days after the local Noorin TV station broadcast a show on Afghan Christians engaging in their rituals. Following diplomatic engagement by governments and human rights groups, Musa was quietly released from prison on February 24, 2011, and reportedly went to Italy, where he is seeking asylum.

Media and Freedom of Expression/Social Freedoms

Afghanistan's conservative traditions have caused some backsliding in recent years on media freedoms, which were hailed during 2002-2008 as a major benefit of the U.S. effort in Afghanistan. In those years, numerous television channels, newspapers, and other media forms were established, giving Afghanistan some of the freest press in the region. Media has expanded to the point where the government has taken steps in 2012 to launch a communications satellite to help with broadcast speed and breadth of dissemination.

However, a press law was passed in September 2008 that gave independence to the official media outlets but also contained a number of content restrictions and required that new newspapers and electronic media be licensed by the government. According to the State Department report on human rights for 2011, there continues to be intimidation and sometimes violence against journalists who criticize the central government or powerful local leaders, and some news organizations and newspapers have occasionally been closed for incorrect or derogatory reporting on high officials.

USAID programs have trained investigative journalists to do more reporting on official corruption and other issues. The United States has provided funding and advice to an Afghan

---

[53] Oppel, Richard Jr. and Abdul Waheed Wafa, "Hazara Minority Hustles to Head of the Class in Afghanistan," *New York Times*, January 4, 2010.

Government Media Information Center that the Afghan government uses to communicate with the public. However, possibly as part of an effort to transition more tasks to the Afghans, or possibly as a sign of frustration with Karzai criticism of some U.S. military operations, U.S. advisers were pulled from the Center in late December 2011.

Separately, Islamic conservatives (such as the Ulema Council, parliamentarian Sayyaf, and Shiite cleric Ayatollah Asif Mohseni), have sometimes asserted control over media content. This has been an attempt to curb the popularity of such post-Taliban networks as Tolo Television. With the Council's backing, in April 2008 the Ministry of Information and Culture banned five Indian-produced soap operas on Tolo Television on the grounds that they are too risqué, although the programs were restored in August 2008 under a compromise that brought in Islamic-oriented programs from Turkey. In 2011, pressure from Islamic conservatives caused Tolo to remove a soap opera called "Forbidden Love." Tolo has also aired programs with women performers—presentations that raise eyebrows among religious conservatives—and about official corruption.

Radio Free Europe/Radio Liberty's "Radio Azadi" service for Afghanistan has distributed 20,000 solar powered radios to poor (and usually illiterate) Afghans to improve their access to information. In general, the government does not restrict access to the Internet, but it does ban access to pornographic web sites.

Regarding broader social freedoms, as another example of the growing power of the Islamist conservatives, alcohol is increasingly difficult to obtain in restaurants and stores, although it is not banned for sale to non-Muslims. There were reports in April 2010 that Afghan police had raided some restaurants and prevented them from selling alcoholic beverages at all. On the other hand, some point to the fact that rock bands have appeared publicly in high profile shows in 2011 as evidence of increasing modernity.

Harsh Punishments

The State Department reports widespread examples of torture, rape, and other abuses by officials, security forces, detention center authorities, and police. In September 2011, U.S. and partner transfers of prisoners to some Afghan facilities were suspended because of alleged torture by Afghan prison authorities. Afghanistan's Interior Ministry and National Directorate of Security denied the allegations, which included assertions that prisoners were being beaten with rubber hoses or given electric shocks. In October 2007, Afghanistan resumed enforcing the death penalty after a four-year moratorium, executing 15 criminals. In August 2010, the issue of stoning to death as a punishment arose when Taliban insurgents ordered a young couple who had eloped stoned to death in a Taliban-controlled area of Konduz Province. Although the punishment was not meted out by the government, it was reported that many residents of the couple's village supported the punishment.

Human Trafficking

For the third year in a row, Afghanistan was again placed in Tier 2: Watch List in the State Department report on human trafficking issued on June 19, 2012 (Trafficking in Persons Report for 2012). However, Afghanistan was given a waiver for an automatic downgrade to Tier 3 (the downgrade is automatic after a country is "watch-listed" for three consecutive years). The waiver was based on a the government's writing of a plan that, if implemented, would qualify as a significant effort to comply with minimum standards for the elimination of trafficking. The government is assessed in the 2012 report as not complying with minimum standards for eliminating trafficking, and not showing evidence of increasing efforts to address the issue.

The State Department report says that women from China, some countries in Africa, Iran, and some countries in Central Asia are being trafficked into Afghanistan for sexual exploitation, although, according to the report, trafficking within Afghanistan is more prevalent than trafficking across its borders. The report asserts that some families knowingly sell their children for forced prostitution, including for *bacha baazi*, a practice in which wealthy men use groups of young boys for social and sexual entertainment. The report added that some members of the Afghan National Security Forces have sexually abused boys as part of the *bacha baazi* practice. The United States has spent about $500,000 to eliminate human trafficking in Afghanistan since FY2001.

Advancement of Women

Women and women's groups are a large component of the burgeoning of civil society in post-Taliban Afghanistan. Freedoms for women have greatly expanded since the fall of the Taliban with their elections to the parliament and their service at many levels of government. The Afghan government pursues a policy of promoting equality for women under its National Action Plan for Women of Afghanistan (NAPWA). The Tokyo Mutual Accountability Framework requires Afghanistan to implement the NAPWA and all of its past commitments and laws to strengthen the rights of women and provide services to them.

The major institutional development since 2001 was the formation in 2002 of a Ministry of Women's Affairs dedicated to improving women's rights, although numerous accounts say the ministry's influence is limited in part because of the relative ineffectiveness of minister Husn Banu Ghazanfar. It promotes the involvement of women in business ventures, and it plays a key role in trying to protect women from domestic abuse by running 11women's shelters across Afghanistan. However, the Afghan government, in January 2011, launched a plan to regulate the shelters by placing them under government control. This has raised concerns that the government might seek to limit the access to the shelters by some women and in some areas. Women's rights groups in Afghanistan expressed outrage over a June 2012 statement by Afghanistan's justice minister that the shelters encourage "immorality and prostitution."

One of the most prominent civil society groups operating in post-Taliban Afghanistan is the Afghanistan Women's Network. It has at least 3,000 members and its leaders say that 75 non-governmental organizations work under its auspices. In addition, the Afghanistan Independent Human Rights Commission (AIHRC) and a private group, Afghanistan Human Rights and Democracy Organization, focus extensively on rights for Afghan women.

Among the most notable accomplishments since 2001, women are performing jobs that were rarely held by women even before the Taliban came to power in 1996, including in the new police force. The first Afghan female pilots arrived for training in the United States in July 2011. There are over 200 female judges and nearly 500 female journalists working nationwide. Women are legally permitted to drive, and press reports say an increasing number of Afghan women, although mainly in Kabul and other main cities, are learning how to drive and exercising that privilege. The wearing of the full body covering called the *burqa* is no longer obligatory, and fewer women are wearing it than was the case a few years ago. In November 2010, the government opened a USAID-funded women-only park in Kabul called "Women's Garden" where women can go, without male escort, and undertake fitness and job training activities.

Some groups, such as Human Rights Watch, report backsliding on women's rights since 2008,[54] although the State Department human rights report for 2011 says that the situation of women in Afghanistan improved "marginally" during 2011. Numerous abuses, such as denial of educational and employment opportunities, continue primarily because of Afghanistan's conservative traditions. This is particularly prevalent in rural areas, and less so in larger urban areas.

- More than 70% of marriages in Afghanistan are forced, despite laws banning the practice, and a majority of brides are younger than the legal marriage age of 16.

- The practice of *baad*, in which women are given away to marry someone from another clan to settle a dispute, remains prevalent,.

- There is no law specifically banning sexual harassment, and women are routinely jailed for *zina*—a term meaning adultery, and a crime under the penal code, and that includes running away from home, defying family choice of a spouse, eloping, or fleeing domestic violence. Under the penal code, a man convicted of "honor killing" (of a wife who commits adultery) cannot be sentenced to more than two years in prison. One case receiving substantial attention in December 2011 has involved a woman who was jailed for having a child outside wedlock even though the child was a product of rape. In order to save face for herself and her family, the woman is contemplating marrying the rapist.

Many Afghan women are concerned that the efforts by Karzai and the international community to persuade insurgents to end their fight and rejoin the political process ("reintegration and reconciliation" process) could result in backsliding on women's rights. Most insurgents are highly conservative Islamists who oppose the advancement of women that has occurred. They are perceived as likely to demand some reversals of that trend if they are allowed, as part of any deal, to control territory, assume high-level government positions, or achieve changes to the Afghan constitution. Karzai has said that these concessions are not envisioned, but skepticism remains, and some Afghan officials close to Karzai do not rule out the possibility of amending the constitution to accommodate some Taliban demands. Women have been a target of attacks by Taliban supporters, including attacks on girls' schools and athletic facilities.

Major Legal Developments

Some Afghan laws passed over the past few years have affected women, both positively and negatively. The Afghan government tried to accommodate Shiite leaders' demands in 2009 by enacting (passage by the National Assembly and signature by Karzai in March 2009) a "Shiite Personal Status Law," at the request of Shiite leaders. The law was intended to provide a legal framework for members of the Shiite minority in family law issues. However, the issue turned controversial when international human rights groups and governments—and Afghan women in a demonstration in Kabul—complained about provisions that would appear to sanction marital rape and which would allow males to control the ability of females in their family to go outside the home. President Obama publicly called these provisions "abhorrent." In early April 2009, taking into account the outcry, Karzai sent the law back to the Justice Ministry for review, saying it would be altered if it were found to conflict with the Afghan constitution. The offending clauses were substantially revised by the Justice Ministry in July 2009, requiring that wives "perform

---

[54] "We Have the Promises of the World: Women's Rights in Afghanistan," Human Rights Watch, December 2009, http://www.wluml.org/sites/wluml.org/files/hrw_report_2009.pdf.

housework," but also apparently giving the husband the right to deny a wife food if she refuses sex. The revised law was passed by the National Assembly in late July 2009, signed by Karzai, and published in the official gazette on July 27, 2009, although it remains unsatisfactory to many human rights and women's rights groups.

On August 6, 2009, perhaps in an effort to address some of the criticisms of the Shiite law, Karzai issued, as a decree, the "Elimination of Violence Against Women" (EVAW) law. Minister of Women's Affairs Ghazanfar told CRS in October 2009 that the bill was long contemplated and not related to the Shiite status law.[55] It was enacted by the National Assembly as a law as of December 2010; it had been held up by the Assembly for final passage because some Islamic conservatives, such as Sayyaf (cited above), reportedly object to the provisions of the law criminalizing child marriages. A U.N. report on human rights in Afghanistan, released January 18, 2012 (A/HRC/19/47), says the EVAW law implementation has been weakened by some Supreme Court rulings and other Afghan legal decisions.

The optimism that greeted the EVAW law was further reduced on March 2, 2012, when the Ulema Council issued a pronouncement saying women should be forced to wear the veil and be forbidden from traveling without a male chaperone. The pronouncement did reiterate support for the rights of women to inherit and own property, and to choose their marital partners. On March 6, 2012, Karzai endorsed the Ulema Council statement.

Women in Key Positions

Despite conservative attitudes, women have moved into prominent positions in all areas of Afghan governance, although with periodic setbacks. Three female ministers were in the 2004-2006 cabinet: former presidential candidate Masooda Jalal (Ministry of Women's Affairs), Sediqa Balkhi (Ministry for Martyrs and the Disabled), and Amina Afzali (Ministry of Youth). Karzai named three women to cabinet posts on January 9, 2010, including Afzali (to Labor and Social Affairs). Of the three, only Afzali was immediately confirmed; the other two (Minister of Health and Minister of Women's Affairs) were kept on in acting capacities and confirmed in subsequent years. Afghanistan has one female ambassador and Karzai has a female deputy chief of staff, Homaira Ludin-Etemadi. In the December 16, 2009, nomination list, Karzai proposed a woman to head a new Ministry of Literacy, but parliament did not vote on this nomination because it had not yet acted to approve formation of the ministry. In March 2005, Karzai appointed a former minister of women's affairs, Habiba Sohrabi, as governor of Bamiyan province, inhabited mostly by Hazaras.

One woman (Masooda Jalal) ran in the 2004 presidential election, and two ran for president in the August 20, 2009, election. In the latter, each received less than one-half of 1%. As noted above, parliamentarian Fawzia Koofi already has declared she will run in 2014, and there are likely to be additional female candidates.

In the National Assembly, the constitution reserves for women at least 17 of the 102 seats in the upper house and 68 of the 249 seats in the lower house of parliament. There were 23 serving in the outgoing upper house, 6 more than Karzai's mandated bloc of 17 female appointees. There were 68 women in the previous lower house (when the quota was 62), meaning 6 were elected without the quota. The number elected in the September 18, 2010, election is 69, one more than

---

[55] CRS meeting with the Minister of Women's Affairs, October 13, 2009.

the quota. (For the election, about 400 women ran—about 16% of all candidates.) The target ratio is ensured by reserving an average of two seats per province (34 provinces) for women—the top two female vote getters per province. (Kabul province reserves 9 female seats.) In the National Assembly, a woman, Shukria Barekzai, was chair of the Defense Committee of the elected lower house during 2011. Some NGOs and other groups believe that the women elected by the quota system are not viewed as equally legitimate parliamentarians.

About 300 women were delegates to the 1,600-person "*peace jirga*" that was held during June 2-4, 2010, which endorsed an Afghan plan to reintegrate insurgents who want to end their fight. The High Peace Council to oversee the reconciliation process, which met for the first time on October 10, 2010, has 9 women out of 70 members, although these women report that their views are not taken into account to any significant extent in the Council. At U.S. and other country urging, a woman was part of the official Afghan delegation to the major international conference on Afghanistan in Bonn on December 5, 2011; she was selected at a meeting of civil society activists in Bonn, a day before the major conference begins.

U.S. and International Posture on Women's Rights

U.S. officials say that its policy is to promote women's rights in Afghanistan rigorously. The Administration has and is following its "Strategy for Assistance to Women in Afghanistan, 2010-2013."[56] U.S. officials said aid allocations are geared toward that strategy. Specific earmarks for use of U.S. funds for women's and girls' programs in Afghanistan are contained in recent annual appropriations, and these earmarks have grown steadily. The United States provided $159 million to programs for Afghan women in FY2009, slightly more than the $150 million earmarked, and about $225 million for FY2010, more than the $175 earmarked.[57] For FY2010, assistance was provided in the following "pillars" of the U.S. Strategy: health ($87 million); education ($31 million); economy, work, and poverty ($54.6 million); legal protection and human rights ($12 million); and leadership and political participation ($43 million). Amounts were similar for FY2011. U.S. funding has been used, in part, to help finance over 830,000 microloans to women during 2004-2011, and they have used these funds to establish 175,000 small businesses, according to the SRAP report released November 2011.

These strategy pillars, and specific programs funded by them, are discussed in annual State Department reports on U.S. aid to women and girls. However, an audit issued in July 2010 by the Special Inspector General for Afghanistan Reconstruction found that the State Department and USAID did not provide complete and consistent information about the reported activities in which women and girls were intended beneficiaries.

The Afghanistan Freedom Support Act of 2002 (AFSA, P.L. 107-327) authorized $15 million per year (FY2003-FY2006) for the Ministry of Women's Affairs. Those monies are donated to the Ministry from Economic Support Funds (ESF) accounts controlled by USAID. S. 229, the Afghan Women Empowerment Act of 2009, introduced in the 111th Congress, would authorize $45 million per year in FY2010-FY2012 for grants to Afghan women, for the ministry of Women's Affairs ($5 million), and for the AIHRC ($10 million).

---

[56] A draft of this strategy document was provided to CRS by the State Department, April 21, 2011.

[57] For prior years, see CRS Report RL30588, *Afghanistan: Post-Taliban Governance, Security, and U.S. Policy*, by Kenneth Katzman, in the section on aid to Afghanistan, year by year.

Democracy, Human Rights, Governance, and Elections Funding Issues

U.S. funding for democracy, governance, and rule of law programs has grown, in line with the Obama Administration strategy for Afghanistan. During FY2002-FY2012, USAID spent about $1.5 billion on democracy, governance, rule of law and human rights, and elections support.

The following was spent by USAID (using Economic Support Funds) for FY2012 and appropriated in P.L. 112-74 (Consolidated Appropriation)

$546.5 million for overall democracy and human rights-related funding including:

- $435.5 million for good governance;

- $31 million for rule of law and human rights (not including INCLE funds);

- $37 million for political competition and consensus building; and

- $43 million for civil society.

For FY2013, the ESF democracy and governance request (ESF) is $578.2 million, including:

- $447.2 million for good governance;

- $31.5 million for rule of law and human rights (not including INCLE);

- $64.3 million for political competition and consensus-building;

- $35.2 million for civil society.

For tables on U.S. aid to Afghanistan, see CRS Report RL30588, *Afghanistan: Post-Taliban Governance, Security, and U.S. Policy*, by Kenneth Katzman.

Effects of a Settlement with the Taliban

A major U.S. and Afghan initiative—to reach a conflict-ending settlement with the Taliban—is likely to affect all of the issues discussed in this paper: Afghan politics, future elections, the performance of the government along all its metrics, and the human rights situation. Many in the international community, including within the Obama Administration, initially withheld endorsement of the concept, fearing it might result in the incorporation into the Afghan political system of insurgent leaders who retain ties to Al Qaeda and will roll back freedoms instituted since 2011. The minority communities in the north, women, intellectuals, and others remain skeptical that their freedoms can be preserved if there is a political settlement with the Taliban. These groups fear that the Taliban could be given major ministries, seats in parliament, or even tacit control over territory as part of any deal. Secretary Clinton said in India on July 20, 2011, that any settlement must not result in and undoing of "the progress that has been made [by women and ethnic minorities] in the past decade." To respond to those fears, Afghan and U.S. officials say that the outcome of a settlement would require the Taliban to drop at least some of its demands that (1) foreign troops leave Afghanistan; (2) a new "Islamic" constitution be adopted; and (3) Islamic law be imposed.

Following the 2010 U.S. shift to supporting a settlement, an "Afghan High Peace Council" intended to oversee the settlement process was established on September 5, 2010. Its 70 members met for the first time under the leadership of senior Northern Alliance figure/former President

Burhanuddin Rabbani on October 10, 2010. Rabbani was appointed because of Karzai's perception that he could bring skeptical Tajiks and other minorities to support reconciliation. These minority figures, as noted above, fear that reconciliation with the Taliban will strengthen Pashtun control of government to the detriment of the non-Pashtun minorities. Rabbani earned substantial respect among all factions for his diligent work in this role; for example he led High Peace Council visits to Pakistan and other regional countries, and established provincial representative offices of the Council in at least 27 provinces. On the other hand, some of the nine women on the Council say their views were routinely dismissed. On September 20, 2011, Rabbani was assassinated by a Taliban infiltrator posing as an intermediary. On April 14, 2012, the High Peace Council members voted Rabbani's son, Salahuddin, as his replacement.

Prior to the Rabbani killing, U.S., Taliban, and Afghan representatives had proliferated. In May 2011, it was reported that U.S. officials had met at least three times in 2011 with Tayeb Agha, a figure believed close to Mullah Umar. In late June 2011, those meetings were confirmed by then-Secretary of Defense Gates, who said the talks had been led by the State Department and have been facilitated by Germany and Qatar. However, the process stalled after the Rabbani assassination and Pakistan's boycott of the December 5, 2011, Bonn Conference over a November 26, 2011, security incident in which U.S. forces killed 24 Pakistani border troops.

In December 2011, as tensions over these issues abated, U.S. officials resumed the process, including pursuing the opening of a Taliban political office in Qatar to facilitate talks. The discussion of a Taliban office in Qatar came amid reports that U.S. officials had been meeting Taliban figures more frequently than was previously believed. The Taliban office has not formally opened to date, but some Taliban figures are operating from Qatar informally, as discussed below. The United States also revealed it had discussed "confidence-building measure" in the form of transferring captives from the Guantanamo detention facility to a form of house arrest in Qatar— to be conducted simultaneous with the Taliban release of the one U.S. prisoner of war, it holds, Bowe Bergdahl. The United States also demanded a public Taliban statement severing its ties to Al Qaeda or other terrorist groups, possibly as a prelude to a limited battlefield ceasefire. There were also discussions of transitioning the talks from U.S.-led to Afghan government-led, although the Taliban was reluctant to undertake such talks because doing so would recognize the government's legitimacy. A release of Taliban captives would require U.S. congressional notification. The Taliban figures to be released to Qatar include some, such as Mullah Mohammad Fazl who were major figures in the Taliban regime (Fazl was deputy defense minister). H.Res. 529 expresses opposition to their release. The confidence-building measures did not take place, and talks stalled in March 2012 reportedly over Qatar's failure to fully assure the United States that the detainees would be able to escape custody. Some U.S. officials say that all sides were not close to serious negotiations on the core issues of any political settlement.

Still, the reconciliation issue appears to be alive and active. An April 15, 2012, attack by militants on several locations in Kabul and other provinces soured the Afghan government on talks, as did the May 2012 assassination of another key intermediary, Arsala Rahmani—a former Taliban official who reconciled with the government and served in the Afghan parliament. But, these were counterbalanced by a February 2012 statement by Pakistani leaders that, for the first time, publicly encouraged Taliban leaders to negotiate a settlement to the conflict. In late June 2012, Afghan government officials and Taliban representatives held talks at two meetings—one in Paris, and one an academic conference in Kyoto, Japan, on reconciliation issues. At the Kyoto meeting, the Afghan government was represented by Mohammad Stanekzai, a member of the High Peace Council, and the Taliban was represented by Din Mohammad, a member of the Taliban political council who had traveled from Qatar. The Kyoto meeting appeared to represent an acceptance by the Taliban of direct talks with Afghan government officials. In August 2012, Afghan officials reportedly held talks with high-ranking Taliban figure Mullah Abdul Ghani Bradar,[58] who was arrested by Pakistan in February 2010, purportedly to halt between Bradar and Afghan intermediaries. Pakistan's decision to grant Afghan officials access to Bradar, at his prison in Pakistan, signaled that Pakistan wants to play a more active role in the reconciliation process. Some Afghan officials express optimism the talks will yield a settlement eventually, particularly if the Afghan government provides assurances of security for Taliban leaders who reconcile.

Table 1. Major Pashtun Tribal Confederations

Clan/Tribal Confederations	Location	Example
Durrani	Mainly southern Afghanistan: Qandahar, Helmand, Zabol, Uruzgan, Nimruz	
Popalzai (Zirak branch of Durrani Pashtun)	Qandahar	Hamid Karzai, president of Afghanistan; Jelani Popal, former head of the Independent Directorate of Local Governance; Mullah Bradar, the top aide to Mullah Umar, captured in Pakistan in Feb. 2010. Two-thirds of Qandahar's provincial government posts held by Zirak Durrani Pashtuns
Alikozai	Qandahar	Mullah Naqibullah (deceased, former anti-Taliban faction leader in Qandahar)
Barakzai	Qandahar, Helmand	Ghul Agha Shirzai (Governor, Nangarhar Province)
Achakzai	Qandahar, Helmand	Abdul Razziq, Police Chief, Qandahar Province
Alozai	Helmand (Musa Qala district)	Sher Mohammad Akhunzadeh (former Helmand governor); Hajji Zahir, former governor of Marjah
Noorzai	Qandahar	Noorzai brothers, briefly in charge of Qandahar after the fall of the Taliban in November 2001
Ghilzai	Eastern Afghanistan: Paktia, Paktika, Khost, Nangarhar, Kunar	
Ahmadzai		Mohammed Najibullah (pres. 1986-1992); Ashraf Ghani, Karzai adviser, Finance Minister 2002-2004
Hotak		Mullah Umar, but hails from Uruzgan, which is dominated by Durranis
Taraki		Nur Mohammed Taraki (leader 1978-1979)
Kharoti		Hafizullah Amin (leader September-December1979); Gulbuddin Hekmatyar, founder of Hezb-e-Islami (Gulbuddin), former *mujahedin* party leader now anti-Karzai insurgent.
Zadran	Paktia, Khost	Pacha Khan Zadran; Insurgent leader Jalaluddin Haqqani

---

[58] "Afghan Officials Meet Key Taliban Figure in Pakistan." Reuters.com, August 12, 2012.

Clan/Tribal Confederations	Location	Example
Kodai		
Mangal	Paktia, Khost	Ghulab Mangal (Governor of Helmand Province)
Orkazai		
Shinwari	Nangarhar province	Fasl Ahmed Shinwari, former Supreme Court Chief Justice
Mandezai		
Sangu Khel		
Sipah		
Wardak (Pashtu-speaking non-Pashtun)	Wardak Province	Abdul Rahim Wardak (Defense Minister)
Afridis	Tirah, Khyber Pass, Kohat	
Zaka khel		
Jawaki		
Adam khel		
Malikdin, etc		
Yusufzais	Khursan, Swat, Kabul	
Akozais		
Malizais		
Loezais		
Khattaks	Kohat, Peshawar, Bangash	
Akorai		
Terai		
Mohmands	Near Khazan, Peshawar	
Baizai		
Alimzai		
Uthmanzais		
Khawazais		
Wazirs	Mainly in Waziristan	
Darwesh khel		
Bannu		

Source: This table was prepared by Hussein Hassan, Information Research Specialist, CRS.

Figure 1. Map of Afghan Ethnicities

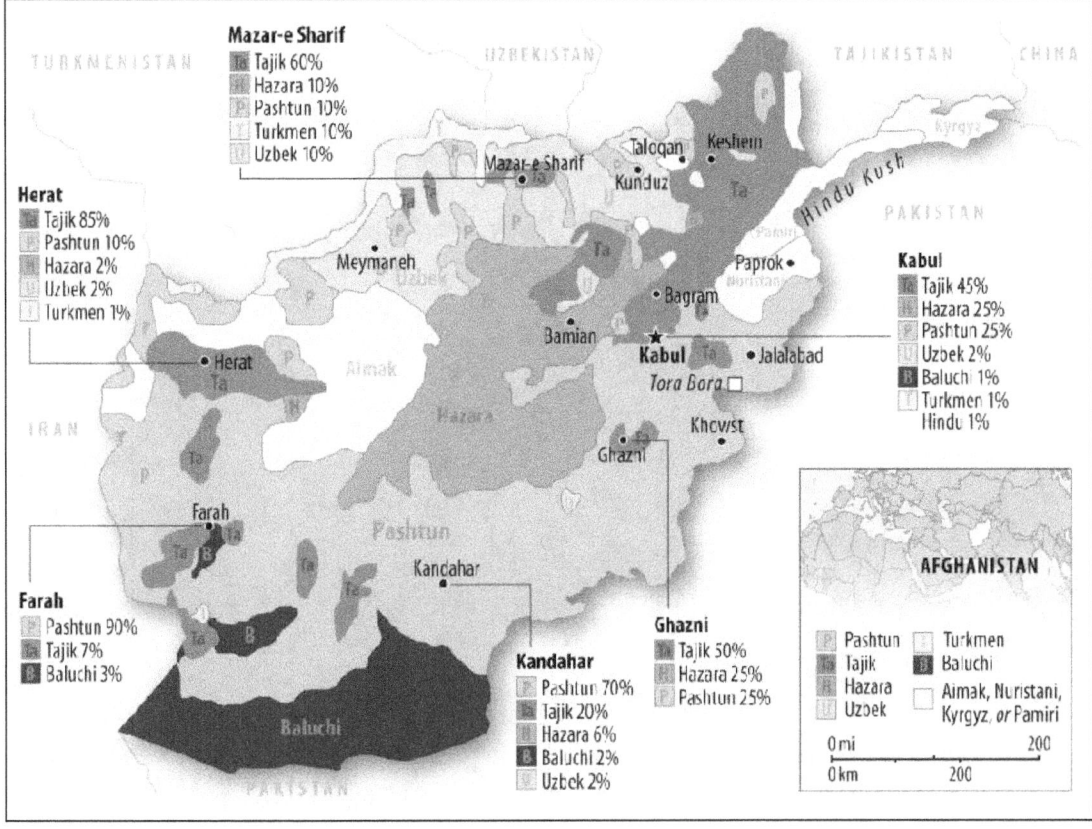

Source: 2003 National Geographic Society, http://www.afghan-network.net/maps/Afghanistan-Map.pdf. Adapted by Amber Wilhelm, CRS.

Notes: This map is intended to be illustrative of the approximate demographic distribution by region of Afghanistan. CRS has no way to confirm exact population distributions.

Author Contact Information

Kenneth Katzman
Specialist in Middle Eastern Affairs
kkatzman@crs.loc.gov, 7-7612

Acknowledgments

The table of major Pashtun tribes was prepared by Hussein Hassan, Information Research Specialist, CRS.